6/02

j500   Everything you need
EVE   to know.

$24.95

DATE			

everything you need to know

an encyclopedia for inquiring young minds

KINGFISHER

BOSTON

...ompany imprint

...etts 02116

...mifflinbooks.com

...ed in 2007

...6 5 4 3 2 1

...7/WKT/SCHOY(SCHOY)/128MA/C

LIBRARY OF CONGRESS CATALOGING-IN-PUBLICATION DATA

Everything you need to know / Deborah Chancellor ... [et al.].—1st ed.

   p. cm.

 Includes index.

 ISBN 978-0-7534-6089-4

1. Science—Juvenile literature. 2. Biology—Juvenile literature. 3.

Technology—Juvenile literature. I. Chancellor, Deborah.

 Q163.E94 2007

 500—dc22

2007004850

AUTHORS:

Deborah Chancellor (Our Earth and My Body chapters)

Deborah Murrell (Dinosaurs, Machines, People and Places, and Space chapters)

Philip Steele (Animals and People Through Time chapters)

Barbara Taylor (Plants and Science chapters)

Editorial manager: Miranda Smith

Managing editor: Carron Brown

Coordinating editor: Stephanie Pliakas

Design manager: Peter Clayman

Designers: Ray Bryant, Emy Manby

Picture research manager: Cee Weston-Baker

Artwork archivists: Wendy Allison, Gina Weston-Baker

Senior production controller: Lindsey Scott

DTP coordinator: Catherine Hibbert

Proofreaders: Susan Buckheit, Sheila Clewley, Polly Goodman

Indexer: Polly Goodman

ISBN 978-0-7534-6089-4

Printed in China

NOTE TO READERS:

The website addresses listed in this book are correct at the time of going to print.
However, due to the ever-changing nature of the Internet, website addresses and
content can change. Websites can contain links that are unsuitable for children.
The publisher cannot be held responsible for changes in website addresses or
content or for information obtained through third-party websites. We strongly
advise that Internet searches be supervised by an adult.

Contents

Dinosaurs

People and Places

People Through Time

My Body

Science

Space

Machines

Using this book

In addition to lots of information, this book has many special features in it to help you enjoy it more. There are facts to amaze, stories for entertaining, vocabulary notepads to expand your word knowledge, difficult questions with fascinating answers, and great activities and games. Enjoy exploring!

▶ Fact box

Look out for the exclamation point on these boxes. Each fact box contains amazing details about the subject matter that is being described. This fact box is from the chapter called "People and Places." You will find it on page 133.

The Kwakiutl people

This tribe, like many other tribes, lived in North America long before Europeans arrived. Many carved tall totem poles like this one to tell the story of their tribe. They celebrated by dancing and wearing masks.

The Tin Man

In the story *The Wizard of Oz*, the Tin Man is sad because he is made of metal and has no heart. He goes in search of one, along with a scarecrow who needs a brain, a lion who needs courage, and a girl named Dorothy who needs to find her way home.

◀ Story box

There are some wonderful stories, fairy tales, and myths in this book. Look out for the "open book" symbol. This story box is from the chapter called "My Body." You will find it on page 208.

VOCABULARY

microphone
An electronic instrument that is used to pick up sound waves that will be broadcast.

factory
A building or group of buildings in which objects are produced in large numbers.

◀ Vocabulary notepad

There are sometimes difficult words used in the text that need further explanations, so there is a notepad especially for this task. This vocabulary notepad is from the chapter called "Machines." You will find it on page 306.

▶ Question circle

Most people have questions that they are dying to ask. You will find circles with questions and their answers in every chapter. This question circle is from the chapter called "Dinosaurs." You will find it on page 104.

WHERE ARE FOSSILS FOUND?

Fossils are usually found where sun, rain, or wind wear away the surrounding rock and expose them.

▶ Can you find?

These features will test what you can spot and name in the pictures. This planet-shaped "Can you find?" is from "Space." You will find it on page 273.

CAN YOU FIND?
1. a comet
2. an asteroid
3. a crater
4. two astronomers
5. the Moon

8

▶ Creative corner

The splotch of paint says it all! This is where you can let your creative self run wild. The book is packed with great things to make and do. This creative corner is from "Animals." You will find it on page 81.

CREATIVE CORNER

Winter food for wild birds

Take half a coconut shell or an empty plastic container. Then ask an adult to melt some shortening or butter in a pan. Mix in seeds, unsalted nuts, oats, cereal, bacon rinds, or cheese. Pour this mixture into the upturned shell or container and leave it to set. Turn the container upside down and hang it up outside, well away from cats.

▼ At the bottom of every right-hand page in the book, you will find one or two useful websites. These have been carefully chosen to add to the information on the page.

▲ You will need:

Plain and colored paper, cardboard (plus tubes), cotton balls, glue, string, rubber bands, scissors, pencils, erasers, modeling clay, crayons, paints, paintbrushes, markers, straws, plastic containers and bottles, wool, tape, potting soil, balloons, tissue paper, pipe cleaners, wooden rods, brass fasteners

Our Earth

As far as we know, Earth is the only planet in the universe with exactly the right conditions for life—and there is an amazing variety of life here. Earth has spectacular landscapes, ranging from icy mountains to lush rainforests to rolling sand dunes.

Our planet

Earth is a planet of incredible extremes—from very hot and dry to cold, wet, or windy. Earth is home to millions of different species that live in a huge variety of habitats. A large habitat is called a biome. Earth's main biomes are desert, grassland, forest, rainforest, tundra, and ocean.

HOW OLD IS EARTH?
Scientists believe that Earth is around 4.5 billion years old and that it was formed from material left behind after the birth of the Sun.

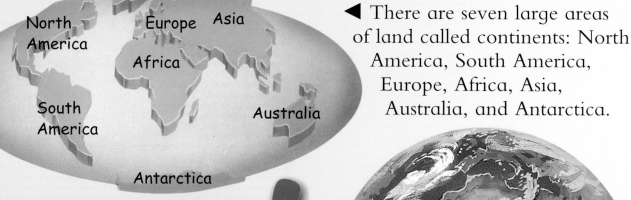

North America
Europe
Asia
Africa
South America
Australia
Antarctica

◀ There are seven large areas of land called continents: North America, South America, Europe, Africa, Asia, Australia, and Antarctica.

Day and night
The Sun lights up one half of Earth, while the other half is dark. When it is daytime in one half of the world, it is night in the other half. Earth is always spinning, and it takes 24 hours to make a complete spin. There is a period of night followed by a period of day.

▲ Earth is a planet in space and is shaped like a ball. Earth looks blue when seen from space because more than two thirds of it is covered with seawater.

► The equator is an imaginary line that runs around the middle of Earth. Places near the equator have a tropical climate (below). Places farther away are cooler, with a temperate climate (right).

VOCABULARY

temperate
A varied climate with four separate seasons each year.

tundra
Frozen and treeless land in countries close to the North Pole.

◄ Africa has large areas of grasslands, also known as savannas, that are home to some amazing wildlife. Giraffes are well adapted to savannas and are able to feed on leafy treetops.

► The pattern of weather in a place over a long period of time is called its climate. Earth has a variety of climates, from the frozen Arctic and Antarctic to the blistering deserts of Africa and Asia.

INTERNET LINKS: www.bbc.co.uk/science/space/solarsystem/earth • www.weatherwizkids.com/climate.htm

▲ Like this jaguar in South America, more than one half of the world's plant and animal species live in rainforests.

Life on Earth

Earth is bursting with life. Over millions of years, animals and plants have slowly adapted to survive in the parts of the world where they now live. This process of change is called evolution. The surrounding living area of a plant or animal is called a habitat. There are many habitats on Earth.

Fear of fire
In an African myth, Kaang, the lord of all life, created the world. He let the people and animals live together on the surface of Earth. But then the people lit fires, which frightened the animals away. After that, the people and animals lived apart.

◄ Rainforests (colored red on this map) are found in tropical areas of the world, near the equator.

Just right for life

Scientists think life began in the oceans around 3.5 billion years ago. Some sea creatures evolved, moving to live on dry land. But many species stayed in the oceans. Some types of marine animals, such as jellyfish, have swum in the oceans for millions of years.

▲ Hot deserts are extremely dry habitats where not many creatures live. Camels are desert animals that are well adapted to the harsh climate. They can survive on very little food or water for as long as seven days.

▼ Ponds are small habitats that are home to animals such as toads and a particular group of plants. These living things depend on one another in a community called an ecosystem.

DO PEOPLE LIVE IN ANTARCTICA?

The only people who live in Antarctica are scientists, and they do not live there all the time. It is the world's coldest and windiest place.

Beneath the surface

The ground under your feet is part of Earth's crust—a layer of solid rock that is 4–43 mi. (6–70km) thick. Under Earth's crust is a layer of hot rock called the mantle. Beneath that is the outer core, a layer of liquid rock. In the center is an iron and nickel ball called the inner core.

Crust
Mantle

Outer core

Continent

Ocean

Inner core

► Fossil fuels, such as coal, oil, and gas, are buried inside Earth's crust. They are drilled out for us to use by oil rigs on land and at sea.

▼ Soil lies near the surface of Earth's crust. It is important for plant growth and provides shelter for animals and insects.

▲ Earth's crust is thin under oceans and thick under mountains. The inner core is very hot, with temperatures of up to 9,000°F (5,000°C).

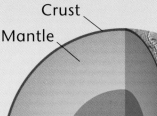

Treasure island
In this story, a boy named Jim Hawkins goes on a voyage to find some buried treasure. A one-legged pirate named Long John Silver joins the search. After many adventures, they find the lost treasure hidden in a cave.

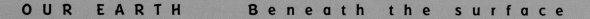

Emerald in rock

Rough emerald

Cut emerald

CAN YOU FIND?
1. a bumblebee
2. a ladybug
3. an ant
4. a butterfly
5. a wren
6. an earthworm

▲ Minerals are hard, natural substances found in rocks in Earth's crust. Rare minerals, such as emeralds, are called gems. They are cut and polished and then made into jewelry.

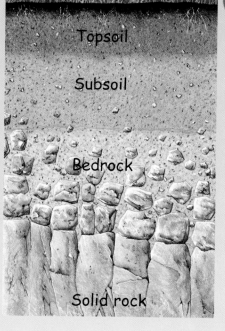

Topsoil

Subsoil

Bedrock

Solid rock

▲ The top layer of soil is the topsoil. Under this layer is subsoil and then small rocks, called bedrock, that lie on solid rock.

CREATIVE CORNER

Colorful soil

Collect some sandy, peaty (moist), and chalky soil. Mix a little of each with water and smear each sample on some white paper. Compare the colors. You will see that different types of soil actually have different colors.

Volcanoes

Earth is a restless planet. Beneath
the crust lies a layer of liquid rock
called magma. This red-hot rock
escapes through weak spots in the
crust, bursting out of volcanoes
both on land and under oceans.
There are around 700 active volcanoes.

**WHERE
IS EARTH'S
LARGEST VOLCANO?**
The massive Mauna Loa
volcano is in Hawaii.
Most of the volcano is
actually under the
Pacific Ocean.

◀ Pressure builds and forces
out the magma through holes
called vents. The erupting
volcano sends up lava and
clouds of thick, dusty ash.

Ash cloud

Hot spring

Red-hot lava

Cooling
lava

Magma
chamber

Vent

Composite volcano

Caldera volcano

Shield volcano

▲ The most common type
of volcano is the composite
volcano. Caldera volcanoes
are the most explosive, and
shield volcanoes can be huge.

Earthquakes

Earth's crust is a loose jigsaw puzzle of plates that slide over the hot rock inside Earth's mantle. Earthquakes happen when the edges of these plates collide, pushing against or away from each other.

▲ A crack in Earth's crust is called a fault line. When two plates collide along a fault line, shock waves are sent out through the surrounding rock, making the ground shake.

▲ Earthquakes may cause buildings to collapse. In countries where earthquakes happen, people practice what to do in an emergency.

▲ Undersea earthquakes can create giant waves called tsunamis. Tsunamis travel at high speeds for many miles. When they finally crash onto the shore, they can cause terrible damage.

Seismograph

An earthquake's vibrations are recorded by an instrument called a seismograph. This very sensitive machine measures the overall strength of an earthquake. The power of an earthquake is described with the Richter scale, numbered from 1 to 9.

The first Chinese seismograph

Mountains and caves

Mountains are made when two plates under Earth's crust push together, forcing up huge folds of rock. Mountains get taller over millions of years, but ice, wind, and weather also wear them down in a process called erosion. Rocky caves are found in mountains and underground.

▲ Glaciers are rivers of ice that move slowly down mountains. When a glacier melts in a valley, it joins a river or makes a new one.

◄ If a mountain has jagged peaks to climb, it is still quite "young." The weather has not had time to smooth down the sharp rock.

Pied Piper
In a German folktale, rats follow the Pied Piper's music out of the town of Hamelin. They are followed by the town's children and all are led to live inside a mountain.

▼ The tallest mountain in each continent is shown below. The world's tallest mountain is Mount Everest.

Everest (Asia)
29,028 ft.

Aconcagau (South America)
22,770 ft.

McKinley (North America)
20,316 ft.

Kilimanjaro (Africa)
19,336 ft.

Elbrus (Europe)
18,506 ft.

Vinson Massif (Antarctica)
16,046 ft.

Kosciusko (Australia)
7,308 ft.

Stalactites and stalagmites

Stalactites grow down from the roof of a cave, and stalagmites grow up from the floor. The world's biggest stalagmite is 230 ft. (70m) tall! There are different types of stalagmites and stalactites.

Drape stalactite   Fir cone stalagmite

Column (both)   Dish stack stalagmite

▶ Dripping water in a cave contains a mineral called calcite. This hardens to form stalagmites and stalactites. The process is very slow— 500 years to grow less than one inch.

HOW BIG IS THE LARGEST CAVE?

The world's biggest cave is around 2,300 ft. (700m) long, 980 ft. (300m) wide, and 230 ft. (70m) high. It is in Sarawak, Malaysia.

Rivers and lakes

A river's journey starts high above sea level, moving quickly downhill. As it nears the coast, it splits into streams and then flows into the ocean. Rivers and lakes give us drinking water, but they contain only one percent of the world's fresh water. The rest is frozen at the poles or trapped underground.

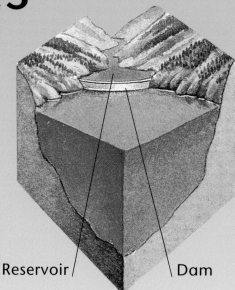

Reservoir / Dam

▼ The Sun's heat turns water in oceans, rivers, and lakes into water vapor, which rises into the sky to form clouds. Water then falls back to the ground as rain. Rainwater collects in rivers, which flow into the ocean. Then the water cycle starts all over again.

? WHY WERE CITIES BUILT NEXT TO RIVERS?
In the past, boats were very important. Cities were built near rivers so that they were easy to reach by boat and trade could happen easily.

▲ Dams are built across rivers to create lakes or reservoirs. Water from dams is used for drinking and also to generate hydroelectric power.

Clouds form

Rain falls

Water evaporates

Rivers flow into the ocean

Queen Isis and the Nile River

The ancient Egyptians believed that the world was made by a god named Ra. Ra crowned his son Osiris king and his daughter Isis queen. When Osiris died, Isis was so heartbroken that her tears flooded the Nile River.

▲ Lakes are big pools of fresh water surrounded by land. Lakes are an important habitat around the world for many living things, including flamingos.

▲ A kayak is a small boat with a two-bladed paddle. Steering a kayak through a fast-flowing river is called white-water kayaking and is a popular watersport.

CREATIVE CORNER

Evaporation experiment

Put a bowl of water outside on a hot, sunny day. Mark the water level. Check the level again that evening. It will be lower, because the sun will have evaporated some of the water.

▲ When a river flows over a cliff or rocky ledge, there is a waterfall. Some waterfalls, such as Niagara Falls in North America, are very spectacular.

Coast (land next to ocean)

Abyssal plain (flat seabed)

Ocean ridge (underwater mountains)

Ocean trench (underwater canyon)

Guyot (underwater island)

Oceans

The vast oceans cover more than one half of Earth, providing a home for more living things than any other habitat. At the bottom of the sea, the ocean floor is a varied and fascinating landscape. Some underwater mountains and canyons are taller and deeper than anything on dry land.

◄ Oceans are shallow near the coast, but farther out there are deep trenches that cut into the ocean floor. Underwater mountain ranges rise up from the depths. Some are thousands of miles long.

Pacific Ocean

CAN YOU FIND?
1. an oil rig
2. an underwater island
3. a tanker
4. an ocean ridge
5. an ocean trench
6. a submarine

▲ There are five main oceans: the Pacific, Atlantic, Indian, Southern, and Arctic. The Pacific is the biggest, and the Arctic is the smallest.

Rocky cliff in a bay

Cave is formed

Cave becomes an arch

Stack is left behind

▲ Ocean meets land at the coast. Waves constantly crash against coastal rocks, and over time this wears away the rocks, changing their shape. This is called erosion.

▲ There are two high tides every day. The Sun and Moon pull on Earth, so the oceans bulge. This makes the water rise, causing high tides.

► Waves are made when the wind blows across the ocean. When a very strong wind blows for a long time, waves can rise as tall as 112 ft. (34m). Surfers make the most of big waves close to the shore.

◄ It is cold and dark on the ocean floor. In volcanic areas, jets of superhot water burst out from underneath Earth's crust. These are called black smokers.

CREATIVE CORNER

An underwater scene
Paint the inside of a shoebox blue. Draw and cut out pictures of sea creatures and hang them from the top of the box, using string and tape. Cover the base with loose sand and small shells.

INTERNET LINKS: www.bbc.co.uk/nature/blueplanet/infobursts.shtml • www.divediscover.whoi.edu/index.html

Air and wind

Earth is surrounded by a blanket of gases called the atmosphere. The atmosphere is very important because it protects us from the sun's dangerous rays and creates the right conditions for life. It also contains the water we drink and the air we breathe.

▼ The atmosphere has five layers. The troposphere, closest to Earth, is where the weather happens. The last layer is the exosphere, up to 560 mi. (900km) above your head!

Exosphere
(300–560 mi.)

Thermosphere
(50–300 mi.)

Mesosphere
(30–50 mi.)

Stratosphere
(7–30 mi.)

Troposphere
(0–7 mi.)

▲ Rising currents of warm air are called thermals. Some birds use thermals to soar and glide. The albatross's huge wingspan of 11.5 ft. (3.5m) helps it glide long distances across oceans.

▲ Air is a mixture of gases, including oxygen. All plants breathe out oxygen. This is why tropical rainforests are so important to Earth and must be saved from destruction.

Calm—Force 0

Breeze—Force 3

Wind—Force 6

Storm—Force 10

◀ Yachts catch the wind in their sails. This propels them forward through the water.

WHY DOES THE WIND BLOW?
When warm air rises, cold air rushes in to take its place. The cold air sinks, sweeping around as it reaches ground level.

▼ Tornadoes are swirling funnels of wind, reaching speeds of up to 250 mph (400km/h). They destroy everything in their path.

▶ Wind is measured with the Beaufort scale, in forces from 0 to 12. A breeze is up to Force 3, a strong wind is Force 6, and a storm is Force 10. A hurricane is Force 12.

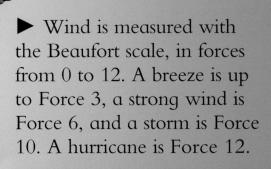

CREATIVE CORNER

Making a windmill
The wind cannot be seen, but you can see it move things. Make a windmill by pinning the corners of four paper triangles together onto a wooden rod. Watch the wind turn the sails of your windmill.

Weather and climate

Weather is made in the troposphere, the part of the atmosphere that is closest to Earth. The air in the troposphere is always changing—it may be moving or still, wet or dry, hot or cold, or a mixture of these things. When air changes, so does the weather. The pattern of weather, or climate, varies around the world.

Freezing climate
Emperor penguins are one of the few species that can survive the freezing climate of Antarctica. The lowest temperature recorded there was −128°F (−89°C)—that is cold enough to shatter steel!

▲ Parts of the world that are close to the equator have heavy rainfall. The rainy season in tropical countries can bring floods, especially in low-lying valleys and plains.

► Clouds form at different heights in the sky. Their shapes can tell you what type of weather is coming. Low stratus clouds may bring rain, and high cirrus clouds may bring snow.

The Snow Queen
In Hans Christian Andersen's fairy tale, a boy named Kay is taken by the evil Snow Queen to her ice palace. Kay's sister, Gerda, travels across the world to rescue him. When Gerda finds Kay, her joyful tears melt his frozen heart, and they return home together.

Cirrus

Key
☐ Polar
☐ Temperate
☐ Cool forest
☐ Desert
☐ Tropical

▲ This map shows the world's climates. The climate in a place is affected by how close it is to the equator, how far it is from an ocean, and how high the land is.

Cumulus

Cumulonimbus

Stratus

The driest desert
Deserts are places where less than 8 in. (20cm) of rain falls each year. The Atacama Desert in Chile is the world's driest desert, because it rains there only a few times every hundred years.

Seasons

It takes one year for planet Earth to travel around the Sun. At different times of the year, one half of the world gets more sunlight than the other half. This means that it is hotter in that half of the world and colder in the other half. The regular rise and fall in temperature around the world is the reason why the seasons change.

◄ The middle of a hurricane is called the "eye" of the storm.

► Hurricanes are powerful storms that reach wind speeds of up to 190 mph (300km/h). They are also known as typhoons and tropical cyclones.

Persephone and the seasons

In a Greek myth, King Hades took Persephone to the underworld to live. Zeus, the king of the gods, said that Persephone could return to the surface if she had not eaten anything in the underworld. She had eaten six pomegranate seeds, so she has to stay for six months every year. During the six months that she is away, there is winter on Earth.

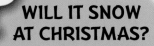

▲ Earth tilts at an angle as it spins and orbits the Sun. It is summer in the half of Earth that leans toward the Sun, and it is winter in the half that leans away from the Sun.

In the spring, the weather warms up and plants begin to grow.

In the summer, the sun shines and it is nice to be outside.

? WILL IT SNOW AT CHRISTMAS?

If you live in the northern half of the world, it may snow at Christmas. But in the south, Christmas is in the summer, so it never snows there at Christmas.

In the fall, it cools down and leaves drop from the trees.

▶ The farther north or south you are from the equator, the farther you are from the Sun's direct heat. The weather is more varied in this temperate climate, and there are four separate seasons: winter, spring, summer, and fall.

In the winter, the weather is cold and the trees are bare.

INTERNET LINKS: www.bbc.co.uk/science/space/solarsystem/earth/solsticescience.shtml

Saving our planet

Earth is an amazing planet, full of life and rich with natural resources. But sadly, we have not cared for our planet. Power plants, factories, and vehicles send gases into the atmosphere, polluting the air. Our world is changing fast, and many species of animals and plants are in danger. We need to do everything we can to save our planet.

▼ Scientists believe that harmful gases in the atmosphere are trapping the sun's heat, making the world warmer. This is known as climate change. All countries must work together to stop climate change from happening.

▲ Many animals, such as orangutans, could soon become extinct because their habitats are being destroyed.

Tiddalik the frog

In an Australian folktale, Tiddalik the frog drank all of the water in the world. A wise wombat told the animals to make Tiddalik laugh. An eel danced, and Tiddalik burst out laughing. Water flowed over Earth again.

▼ Bikes are fun to ride, and they do not pollute the air. Ride your bike or walk on short trips, instead of going by car.

▲ Remember to sort your garbage carefully before it is thrown away. Glass, aluminum, paper, and some plastics can be recycled. When a material is recycled, it is processed so that it can be used again. This saves Earth's precious resources.

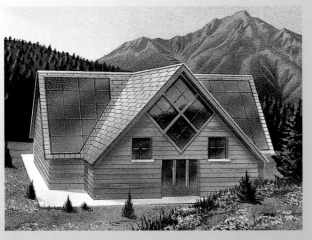

▲ Solar power uses the sun's heat and light to make electricity. This is good for the environment because it is clean. Our energy mostly comes from fossil fuels, such as oil and coal, which create pollution.

CREATIVE CORNER

Making a junk model

Think about whether you can use something again before you throw it away. Boxes, cartons, and packaging materials can be used to make excellent models. Try making a model of a robot from some of your trash.

INTERNET LINKS: www.epa.gov/climatechange/kids • www.panda.org/

Now you know!

▲ More than two thirds of planet Earth is covered with seawater. The large areas of land are called continents.

▲ Our Earth is a restless planet. Movements and pressures under Earth's crust make volcanoes erupt and earthquakes happen.

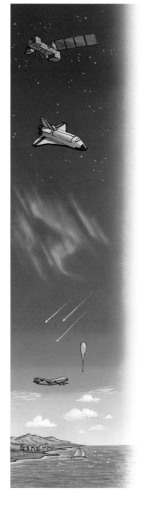

▲ Earth is protected by a blanket of gases, which is called the atmosphere. The air that we breathe is in the atmosphere, and the weather is made there, too.

▶ The water that we drink comes from rivers, lakes, and reservoirs. It is always being recycled in a natural process called the water cycle.

▲ The environment of a living thing is called its habitat. There are many different habitats on Earth.

▲ Weather is made by changes and movements in the air. Climate is the pattern of weather that happens in a place over a long period of time.

▲ Many living things are in danger of dying out, and pollution is warming our climate. We must all keep Earth clean and safe.

Plants

From tiny tomato plants to gigantic trees, plants are vitally important to life on Earth because they make their own food. All animals have to eat plants or other animals that have eaten plants. As well as using plants for food, people also rely on them for clothing, medicine, and fuel.

What are plants?

From tiny mosses to giant trees, plants are living things that make their own food. Animals cannot do this, so they rely on plants to keep them alive. Like animals, plants breathe, reproduce, and grow. Plants grow throughout their lives.

Flower animals
Some animals look like plants. This sea anemone looks like a flower, but it is really an animal. It catches fish and other small creatures in its stinging tentacles.

Leaves trap sun's energy

◀ Plants use the sun's light energy to make sugars from water and a gas in the air called carbon dioxide. This happens mostly in the leaves of a plant.

Sugars go to rest of plant

Oxygen is released

Leaves take in carbon dioxide

Roots take in water

▶ There are more than 400,000 plants in the world, divided into two groups. One group grows from spores and includes ferns, seaweeds, and mosses. The other grows from the seeds made inside flowers or cones.

Water pipes

Food pipes

▲ Inside a plant's stem are rows of pipes that carry food and water around the plant. Water travels up the plant, from the roots to the leaves. Food travels both up and down the plant.

Inside a tree trunk you will find growth rings—one for each year of the tree's life.

? **WHAT ARE FUNGI?**
Fungi, such as these mushrooms and toadstools, are living things that are neither plants nor animals. But, like some plants, they grow from spores.

Seedless plants

Plants such as seaweeds, mosses, and ferns do not have flowers, so they cannot make seeds. Instead, they produce new plants by releasing small spores. In order for spores to develop, these plants need water, so they grow in damp places or in water.

▼ Most moss plants grow low to the ground in cushions, clumps, tufts, or flat mats. They have thin stems, simple leaves, and no true roots.

VOCABULARY
cell
A microscopic unit from which all living things are made.
spore
A tiny package of cells used in reproduction, when new plants are created.

Lichens are algae and fungi living together

▲ Liverworts belong to the same group of plants as mosses. They often grow on top of the soil.

1. Spores form in sacs

2. Fern releases spores

3. New fern plant grows

▲ Ferns produce spores in sacs under their leaves. A large fern may produce several hundred million spores in one year.

Amazing algae

Algae have no roots, leaves, or flowers. But seaweeds, such as this kelp with a sea lion swimming through it, have leaflike fronds. They also have stalks called stipes and rootlike "holdfasts" that cling to the ground. Most algae live in water.

▶ Millions of years ago, some horsetails grew as tall as trees. Today they are small plants that are around as tall as poppies.

CREATIVE CORNER

Dinosaur world

Make a fern world for toy dinosaurs in a seed tray. Grow carrot tops in some water in saucers. Then, when they grow, plant them in a layer of potting soil in the tray. You could also add garden mosses or ferns from a plant center.

Fungi

Fungi are not plants because they cannot make their own food. They absorb their food from other living things or dead remains. Fungi don't have roots, stems, or leaves. We notice them only when they produce mushrooms or toadstools for spreading the spores that grow into new fungi.

4. Spores fall from gills under cap

1. Spores grow threads called hyphae

3. Mushroom grows bigger

2. Threads weave to make a mycelium

◀ Mushrooms grow from a clump of woven threads called a mycelium. The threads pack together to make mushrooms. These push up above the ground.

Fairy rings
Some fungi, such as the fairy ring mushroom, grow in a circle. They often appear overnight. This made people think that the mushrooms were magic circles where fairies danced. Fairy rings form from an underground mycelium of threads that grows in a circle.

◀ Fungi can survive in caves because they do not need light to make food. They live on animal droppings and dead animals.

WHICH FUNGI HELP DOCTORS?

Some fungi produce chemicals called antibiotics, which help fight diseases. The most famous is a mold called penicillium, used in the production of the drug penicillin.

▲ Fungi are important in the natural world because they convert dead material into forms that other living things can use. This is natural recycling.

▶ Microscopic fungi called yeasts are used to make wine and beer. The bubbles of carbon-dioxide gas that they produce make bread rise.

CREATIVE CORNER

Spore prints

Cut off the stalk of a mushroom, lay it onto a piece of paper, and then cover it with a bowl. Leave it for 24 hours and then take a look. The spores will have formed a print of the mushroom on the paper.

Seed plants

Many plants grow from seeds, which are made inside cones or flowers. Inside a seed is a baby plant. A hard, waterproof coat called a testa protects it. The seed takes in moisture, the case splits open, and roots and shoots sprout. When the seed has grown leaves, it can start to make its own food and continue to grow.

▼ Seeds grow in the middle of flowers. These develop into fruit and nuts. The seeds of plants with cones are tucked inside the scales of the female cones such as those in the cones of the larch tree.

The first root pushes down

More roots appear

A green shoot pushes upward

▲ When a bean seed starts to grow, the roots appear first. Next, a green shoot begins to grow upward, toward the light. When it is above the ground, the shoot grows green leaves.

Horse chestnut leaf and flowers

Larch branch with cone

Acorn

► A greenhouse lets in light through the glass so that plants can grow. It keeps out the wind and traps heat, making plants grow faster.

Fantastic fruit

The world's biggest fruit comes from the coco-de-mer, a palm tree that grows on the Seychelles islands in the Indian Ocean. The fruit weighs up to 44 lbs. (20kg) and takes five to ten years to ripen. Inside are only two or three seeds.

1. Poppy flowers are folded up inside buds

2. Bees bring yellow pollen dust from other poppy flowers

▶ When seeds develop in a poppy, the petals fall off. The middle of the flower swells into a "pepper pot" with holes around the top. The tiny black seeds are shaken out of the holes by the wind.

3. Seeds develop and are shaken out by the wind

Once above the ground, the shoot grows leaves

CREATIVE CORNER

Watercress people

After eating a hard-boiled egg, keep the eggshell. Gently scrape the inside clean, wash it, and then put some wet cotton balls or paper at the bottom. Sprinkle in some watercress seeds. Paint a face on the eggshell and wait for the watercress "hair" to grow!

INTERNET LINKS: www.bbc.co.uk/gardening/gardening_with_children/homegrownprojects_salad.shtml

Plants with cones

Most of the plants that produce their seeds in cones are trees called conifers. Many of the cones are woody, but some, such as juniper cones, look like berries. Most conifers are evergreen, which means that they have leaves all year round.

► Conifer leaves may be flat and narrow or look like needles or scales. If conifer bark is damaged, a sticky substance called resin usually oozes out to protect and seal the wound.

▼ The seeds inside cones provide a useful source of food for animals. The "crossed" bill of the crossbill is perfect for opening the scales of pinecones to reach the seeds.

The largest trees
The redwood tree family from North America includes the world's biggest trees. They can grow more than 260 ft. (180m) high and measure up to 100 ft. (30m) around the base of the trunk. The thick, red, spongy bark of redwoods helps them survive the heat of forest fires.

Silver fir

Cedar of Lebanon

Male cone   Female cone   Ripe female cone

▲ Each conifer produces male and female cones. The male cones make pollen, and the female cones produce seeds. In warm weather, the ripe female cones open and the winged seeds float away on the wind.

VOCABULARY
cone
A tight cluster of modified leaves. The seeds inside a cone may take up to three years to ripen.

▲ Yew trees are part of the conifer family, but they do not produce true cones. Their seeds develop inside red, fleshy cups called arils.

Ginkgo

Ancient plants
Ginkgo trees and cycads are grouped with conifers because they produce seeds but do not have flowers. Cycads have cones, but ginkgo seeds grow inside fleshy fruit. Both plants have been growing on Earth for hundreds of millions of years. Their ancestors were alive when dinosaurs roamed Earth.

Cycad

Stone pine

Coastal redwood

Italian cypress   Phoenician juniper   Norway spruce

Flowering plants

The job of a flower is to make seeds. Before seeds can develop, pollen (a yellow dust that contains male sex cells) has to join with female egg cells. Most flowers rely on the wind or animals to bring pollen from another flower of the same type.

? HOW LONG DO PLANTS TAKE TO FLOWER?
Most plants flower every year or every two years. The slowest flowering plant is *Puya raimondii*, which takes 150 years to flower and then dies.

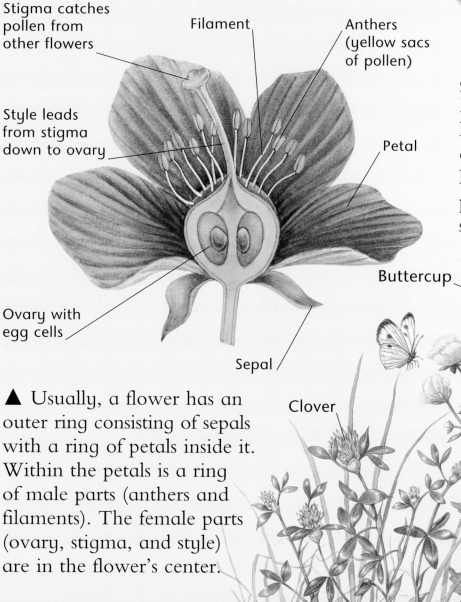

Stigma catches pollen from other flowers

Filament

Anthers (yellow sacs of pollen)

Style leads from stigma down to ovary

Petal

Ovary with egg cells

Sepal

Clover

Buttercup

Corn marigold

▼ There are two main groups of flowering plants. Monocots have narrow leaves, flower parts in threes, and seeds that sprout one leaf. Dicots have flower parts in fours or fives. Their seeds sprout two leaves.

▲ Usually, a flower has an outer ring consisting of sepals with a ring of petals inside it. Within the petals is a ring of male parts (anthers and filaments). The female parts (ovary, stigma, and style) are in the flower's center.

Wind power

Some flowers, such as these hazel catkins, use the wind to carry their pollen from flower to flower. Wind-pollinated flowers are small and dull colored. They do not have to attract insects to carry the pollen.

▶ Can you see the yellow pollen dust on this bee? When the bee visits another foxglove, some of the pollen sticks to the female parts of the flower. This transfer of pollen is called pollination.

Pollen dust

Sac of pollen

Bird's-eye primrose

Nettle-leaved bellflower

Daisy

Sea holly

Saint John's wort

Crocus

▲ Some plants have one flower on the end of a long stem. Other flowers, such as primroses, are grouped together in flower heads.

Knapweed

Poppy

CREATIVE CORNER

Flower pressing

Lay a sheet of paper onto some thick cardboard. Position some flowers so that they do not touch. Put a second piece of paper on top and then some heavy books. Leave the flowers for two weeks or until they are dry. Lift out the flowers and use them to make cards.

How seeds spread

Plants spread their seeds in four main ways. Some seeds are blown away by wind or washed away by water. Other plants throw out their own seeds, although they do not travel very far. Many plants use animals to help them spread their seeds.

▲ Squirting cucumbers burst open and fling out their seeds. The seeds may travel several feet before they fall to the ground.

▼ When birds eat fruit, the seeds that they swallow pass through their bodies. They come out in their droppings, which are deposited away from the plant that made the seeds.

VOCABULARY
fruit
Part of a plant that grows from the flower and contains the seed or seeds.
nut
A hard, dry fruit with one seed inside. Many trees grow nuts.

▶ Some seeds stick to the coats of animals, such as this maned wolf, when they brush against the plants. The seeds may be carried a long way before they fall off.

▲ Dandelion flowers produce many seeds, each with a fluffy "parachute" on top. The parachutes catch the wind, and the seeds float away.

▶ Seeds from fleshy fruit are often spread by animals that eat them. The fruit may have bright colors or shiny surfaces to attract the animals. The tough seed walls protect the seeds when they are eaten.

CREATIVE CORNER

Helicopter seeds

Some seeds, such as lime seeds, spin when they fall. Make your own "helicopter" seed by cutting the shape below out of thin cardboard. Cut along the dotted lines. Stick some modeling clay on the bottom to give it weight. Fold the blades up at point A and down at point B. Then throw the seed up into the air and watch it spin to the ground.

WHY DO ANIMALS BURY NUTS?

Animals such as squirrels and jays bury nuts as a supply of food for the winter. They often store more than they need. The spare nuts might then grow into new plants.

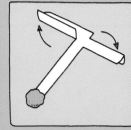

INTERNET LINKS: www.mbgnet.net/bioplants/seed.html

Broad-leaved trees

Broad-leaved trees have wide, flat leaves and flowers that develop into fruit that encloses its seeds. Many broad-leaved trees, such as oak and apple trees, are deciduous. This means that they lose their leaves in the fall or during a dry season. Others, such as holly trees, are evergreen. They have leaves all year round.

Roots
Some trees, such as the fig (right), have very long roots in order to reach water hidden deep underground. Rainforest trees (below) take up nutrients from the soil's surface with shallow roots.

▼ Older, tougher roots are used mostly for anchoring trees, while younger, thinner roots take in water and minerals from the soil.

▶ In places with cold winters, deciduous trees lose their leaves. They cannot take up enough water from the frozen soil.

Oak tree in the summer

► There are two main types of leaves on broad-leaved trees. Simple leaves have one leaf blade at the end of a stalk. Compound leaves are made up of several small leaflets growing on the same stalk. Wide, flat leaves have a big surface area for making food.

Cherry

Hickory

Horse chestnut

Oak

Holly

White willow

► Every year, a tree grows a new ring of wood under the outer layer of its bark. When a tree is cut down, you can tell the age of the tree by counting the rings inside its trunk.

CREATIVE CORNER

Leaf pictures

Collect your favorite leaves. Press them (see "Flower pressing" on page 45) and let them dry naturally. Now you can glue the leaves onto paper in a pattern to make pictures. Try making pictures of different trees.

Oak tree in the winter

INTERNET LINKS: http://forestry.about.com/library/treekey/bltree_key_id_start.htm

Rainforest plants

Rainforests grow around the middle of Earth (the equator), where it is hot and wet all year round. Plants grow well in this environment. Rainforests are home to at least one half of all plant species in the world. Since there are no seasons, rainforest trees are evergreen.

Layers of life

Rainforests grow in several layers. Most life is found in the top layer, called the canopy, which receives the most rain and sunlight. Between the canopy and the forest floor is an understory. Here there are smaller trees, climbing plants, and large-leaved shrubs that can grow in the shade. The forest floor is dark and covered with a carpet of leaves.

▲ Some plants grow on the branches of rainforest trees, where they are closer to the sunlight. These plants are epiphytes, and most of them do not harm the trees on which they perch.

► Towering rainforest trees are 100–160 ft. (30–50m) tall. Their leafy tops form a green roof on the forest. Climbing plants twist around their trunks, and their roots help hold the soil together.

Tarzan of the apes

The author Edgar Rice Burroughs created a character named Tarzan who was raised by apes in the depths of the African jungle. Tarzan became the king of his ape tribe and had many adventures swinging through the trees.

Rainforest plants have thick leaves with pointed tips that help the rain drip off easily.

▶ Epiphytes called tank plants have a watertight cup of waxy leaves that holds many gallons of water. Animals, such as frogs, use these treetop pools as nurseries.

CREATIVE CORNER

Making a bottle garden

Put a layer of gravel in a large, open-necked bottle and add compost. Now put in some plants. Add moss and sticks to make it look like a forest floor. Pour in a cupful of water before putting on the cap. You will not have to water your garden again.

Water plants

Many plants grow in the fresh water of ponds and rivers and in the salty water of oceans. Water plants are surrounded by nutrients, but may find it hard to get enough light or oxygen. Some water plants float freely, while others are rooted in the mud or attached to rocks.

▲ In the fresh water of ponds and lakes, there are many water plants, including lilies, reeds, and willow trees. Insects and animals need water plants to give them food and shelter and to make oxygen.

WHICH PLANTS FLOAT ON WATER?

Duckweeds often cover the water's surface. Their leaves float on the water, absorbing light and making food. Their roots hang under the water, taking in nutrients.

▼ The very smallest plants of all are types of algae, and you can see them only through a microscope. They float in lakes and oceans and are called phytoplankton.

▲ Mangrove trees grow in swamps where there is not much oxygen in the mud. Special roots grow above the mud and take in oxygen from the air.

VOCABULARY

seaweed
A plant that grows in the salty water of the ocean.

mangrove
A tropical tree that grows in marshes or close to the ocean.

◄ The giant water lily from the rivers of the Amazon rainforest grows huge leaves that are strong enough to hold the weight of a small child.

Oarweed

◄ Green seaweeds live near the surface of the ocean, while red and brown seaweeds live at greater depths.

Dulse   Thongweed

Carrageen

Serrated wrack

INTERNET LINKS: http://42explore.com/pond.htm

Desert plants

Plants find it difficult to survive the lack of water in a desert. Desert plants have deep or wide-spreading roots to collect as much water as possible. They may also store water in swollen stems or underground roots.

▲ Pebble plants are made of two fleshy leaves that are full of water. They look like stones so that animals do not eat them.

▼ Deserts are very hot places, so many of the animals that live there come out only at night. During the day, the tiny elf owl hides inside the giant cactus, where it is cooler. It comes out to hunt when it is dark.

CAN YOU FIND?
1. an elf owl
2. a Gila woodpecker
3. a saguaro cactus
4. a rattlesnake
5. a kit fox
6. a roadrunner chasing a lizard

▶ Date palms grow well in desert oases, which are natural springs of water in a dry desert. The water in the oases may come from distant mountains and flow underground through the rocks until it comes to the surface in the desert.

▲ Some plants survive long periods of time as seeds buried in desert sand. When it rains, they quickly flower and produce seeds. When a cactus flowers, water escapes from its petals, so they flower for only a few days each year.

Cactus lunch
The land iguana (a large lizard) lives in desertlike parts of the Galápagos Islands in the Pacific Ocean. It feeds mostly on the prickly pear cactus, breaking off the cactus spines before swallowing the juicy stems. The spines of a cactus are really its leaves. They do not lose water as easily as wide, flat leaves.

INTERNET LINKS: www.desertusa.com/flora.html

Meat-eating plants

Some plants trap insects and other small animals. This meat provides these plants with the extra nutrition that they need in order to survive in poor soil. Plant traps include leaves full of water, sticky leaves, or spiny leaves that snap shut like an animal's jaws.

? HOW MANY MEAT-EATING PLANTS ARE THERE?
More than 600 different types have been identified so far. There are many more waiting to be discovered.

◀ After trapping insects, this pitcher plant slowly dissolves their bodies to make a soupy meal. The pitcher plant then soaks up the meal through its leaves.

▲ Insects land on the leaves of Venus flytraps to eat the sweet nectar that is produced. If they brush against sensitive trigger hairs on the inside of each leaf, the trap snaps shut. It closes in an amazing one third of a second!

A habitat for meat-eating plants

Meat-eating plants live worldwide, from cold peat bogs and flooded grasslands to hot, tropical rainforests. Peat bogs, like this one, form over thousands of years as lakes are gradually filled in with mud and plants.

▼ The leaves of sundew plants are covered with special hairs that have drops of "glue" on the ends. Insects are attracted to the shiny drops, but they become stuck when they land.

CREATIVE CORNER

Dangerous gardening

Buy some meat-eating plants at a plant center. Ask how they should be cared for. Put them in your bedroom or kitchen to catch flies and other insects.

Useful plants

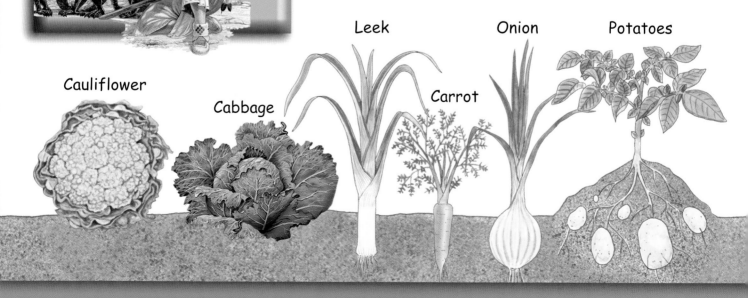

From food and clothing to fuel and medicine, plants are very useful to people. For example, the wood from trees is used for building, and the stems of the rattan palm tree are shaped to make cane furniture, baskets, and ropes.

The first people

A traditional Native American legend tells how the first people were black and scaly and lived underground. A priest named Yanauluha taught them how to grow plants, make medicine, and live on the surface of Earth.

► Spices are made from the flowers, fruit, stems, roots, and seeds of plants. Some spices are very hot, while others are sweeter.

▼ Fruit and vegetables are an important part of a healthy diet. Eating five servings of fruit and vegetables each day will keep your body working well.

Leek

Onion

Potatoes

Carrot

Cauliflower

Cabbage

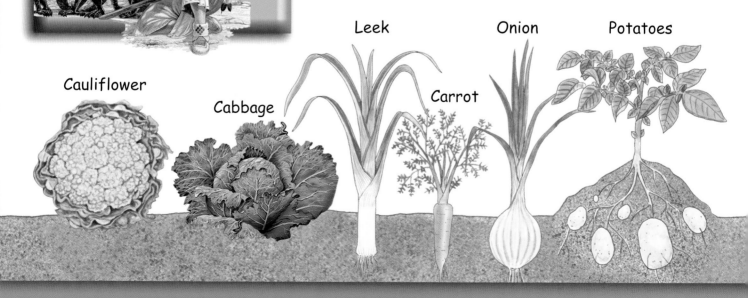

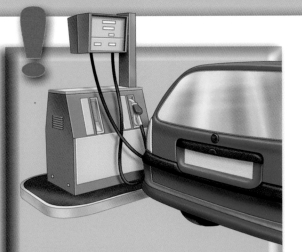

Plants for fuel

Some plants can be made into a type of fuel that can be used instead of gasoline to power car engines. Gasoline is made from oil, which will run out in the future. Plant fuel will not run out. The problem is that it takes a lot of land to grow the plants, so forests are cut down to make space.

Rosy periwinkle, a treatment for leukemia

Aloe, a treatment for burns

Foxglove, a treatment for heart disease

▲ Before modern medicines were invented, people used plants only to treat illnesses and diseases. Many of the modern remedies still use plant products.

▼ Apples and other fruit may be picked by hand before going to stores to be sold. Other plants, such as the fluffy cotton used to make clothes, may be harvested using big machines.

CREATIVE CORNER

Growing an herb garden

Choose seeds of herbs that you like to eat. Plant them in pots inside your home, pressing them firmly into the soil. Water from beneath. When the plantlets are half an inch high, transplant them to a large pot or window box outside.

INTERNET LINKS: http://sustainable.tamu.edu/slidesets/kidscompost/kid1.html

Unusual plants

The plant world is amazing. It includes the biggest and oldest living things, plants that glow in the dark, and seeds that sprout after thousands of years. The most amazing fact is that animals and people would not be able to live in a world without plants.

▼ Bamboo is the fastest-growing plant. It can grow 35 in. (90cm) in one day. Sometimes creaking can be heard as the plant grows upward.

◄ The largest living things are the giant redwood trees of North America. The biggest is more than 260 ft. (80m) tall and more than 2,000 years old.

Two-leaf wonder

The Welwitschia mirabilis plant grows only two leaves, which are 6.5–26 ft. (2–8m) long and tear into thinner strips with age. Dew collects under the leaves, helping the plant survive in the Namib Desert of Africa. The plant lives for 400 to 1,500 years.

◄ The biggest flower belongs to the rafflesia plant of Southeast Asia. The flower is up to 3 ft. (1m) across and smells like rotting meat.

Plants in danger

At least one out of every eight plant species is in danger of dying out, or becoming extinct. People are the main cause of plant extinctions. Habitat destruction, chemical poisoning, and climate change are threatening the survival of many plants.

▲ The biggest danger to plants is the destruction of their habitats such as by cutting down forests for timber and draining wetlands to build houses.

▲ Bee orchid plants are threatened by people turning grassland habitats into farmland. By doing this, they dig up plants and damage young shoots by trampling on them.

Saving plants

To save the world's rare plants, scientists need to find out which plants are endangered. They must plan ways to protect and manage habitats. Rare plants can also be grown in botanical gardens or preserved in seed banks. Some plants can be reintroduced into the wild.

INTERNET LINKS: http://library.thinkquest.org/27257/rafflesia.html • www.plantzafrica.com/plantwxyz/welwitschia.htm

Plants at home

All types of plants can be grown in pots, window boxes, hanging baskets, and gardens. Plants are grown from seeds, but they can also be grown from pieces of older plants, such as cuttings, bulbs, or stems, that sprout new plants. To grow well, plants need light, air, water, and warmth. However, different plants need different growing conditions.

▲ Ladybugs are good for gardens because they eat greenflies, which suck the sap from plants.

▼ Wild plants like these attract wildlife such as butterflies and birds. Climbing plants provide shelter for snails, and birds may nest among the leaves.

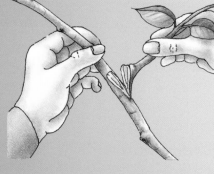

◀ Woody shrubs and trees can be grown from cuttings taken in the fall. Some shrubs root more easily if the cutting has a sliver of wood from the main stem.

Jack and the beanstalk

In an English tale, Jack trades a cow for some magic beans, which grow into a huge beanstalk. Jack steals gold coins, a hen that lays golden eggs, and a harp from a giant at the top of the beanstalk. The giant chases Jack, but Jack chops down the beanstalk and the giant falls to his death.

▲ Hanging baskets are good places to grow trailing plants. The baskets need to be watered frequently because they dry out quickly.

◀ A bulb consists of an underground stem and a bud, which is surrounded by leaves that are full of stored food. Flowers, such as hyacinths and daffodils, grow in the spring using food stored in bulbs.

▲ You can grow wild plants or herbs from seeds, or flowers from bulbs, in a window box or in pots for a patio. The containers need to have drainage holes in the bottom.

CREATIVE CORNER

Growing plants from cuttings

Take cuttings from plants during the summer months. Cut off the tips of side shoots or young stems without flowers. Gently pull off the lower leaves and plant the cuttings in soil or peat-free compost. When the cuttings grow roots, they will be able to develop into new plants.

INTERNET LINKS: www.bbc.co.uk/gardening/gardening_with_children/plantstotry_easy1.shtml

Now you know!

▲ Some plants, such as mosses and ferns, reproduce using spores instead of seeds. Spores are smaller and simpler.

▲ Many plants produce their seeds in flowers. Some plants produce their seeds in cones.

▲ Plants use the energy in sunlight to make their own food from water and carbon dioxide. Animals and fungi cannot do this.

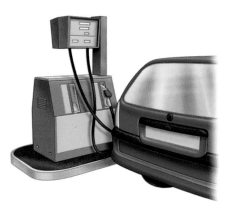

▲ There are more different types of plants living in rainforests than in any other place in the world.

▲ When a tree is cut down, you can tell its age by counting the rings inside the trunk.

▲ Plants spread their seeds using wind, water, or animals. Some plants throw out their own seeds, but they do not go very far.

▶ A few plants trap insects for extra food. They trap the animals by using sticky leaves, spikes, or leaves full of water.

▲ People use plants for all types of purposes, including building houses, flavoring food, treating illnesses, and making cars move.

Animals

Animals are living beings. They have developed
in different forms that can survive on almost
every part of the planet—on land, in oceans,
or in the air. They include everything from the
tiniest insect to the largest whale, flying beetles
and squeaking bats, colorful parrots, monkeys,
apes—and humans, too.

What is an animal?

There are around ten million different animal types, or species, living on Earth today. Animals are life forms that are made up of tiny units called cells. Animals can take in life-giving oxygen from air or water. They can move from one place to another. They can take food inside their bodies and digest it.

CAN YOU FIND?
1. flying animals
2. the biggest eye
3. the longest neck
4. water animals
5. the biggest animal
6. the fastest animal

African elephant

Butterfly

Falcon

▼ Animals can live in all types of places. Some can swim in water or fly in the air, while others live on land. Animals with backbones are called vertebrates. Boneless animals are called invertebrates.

Giraffe

Ostrich

Whale shark

Spider

Snake

Extinct animals

Animals have developed, or evolved, over millions of years. Some species have died out, or become extinct. The dodo was a turkey-size pigeon that lived on islands in the Indian Ocean. It was hunted for food and became extinct around 1680.

The first animals

A very old story from Sierra Leone in Africa tells how God made spare skins for humans so that they could survive death. God ordered Dog to take these skins to the humans, but on the way Dog fell asleep and Snake stole all of the skins. This is why snakes can now change their skins, whereas humans die when they get old—and why many people do not like snakes.

Albatross

Blue whale

Giant squid

Crocodile

Cheetah

Soft bodies, hard shells

Mollusks are invertebrates with soft bodies. Some have hard shells. Mollusks include slugs, snails, all types of shellfish, squids, and octopuses. Crustaceans are armor-plated invertebrates. They include crabs, lobsters, and wood lice.

WHEN DO SNAILS CLOSE UP?
During cold winters, snails may seal up their shells with a chalky substance and wait for the spring and warmer weather to come.

VOCABULARY

invertebrate
An animal that does not have a backbone or spinal column.

crustacean
An animal that lives mostly in water and has a hard shell and jointed limbs.

▼ Many mollusks and crustaceans live on seashores and in rock pools, alongside other sea creatures such as starfish.

Crab

Octopus

Starfish

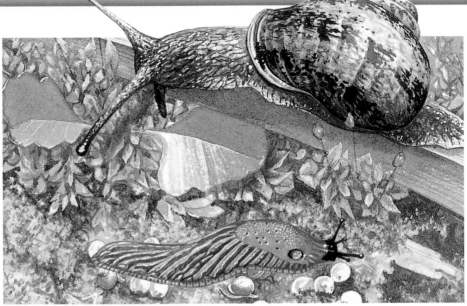

▲ Wood lice like to live in damp, dark places. They may often be found under rotting logs or stones. They have seven pairs of legs.

▲ Snails are found on land, in ponds, and in oceans. They carry shells on their backs and can pull back inside the shells if they are threatened. Most slugs have no shells outside their bodies.

Lobster

The hermit crab

The hermit crab is a crustacean. Instead of having its own body armor, it squeezes inside the empty shell of a mollusk. This hermit crab has found its new home in the shell of a whelk.

INTERNET LINKS: www.kiddyhouse.com/snails/ • www.enchantedlearning.com/subjects/ocean/

Butterfly eggs

Caterpillar

Chrysalis

Insects

There are around one million insect species in the world, including flies, butterflies, bees, crickets, ants, and beetles. Insects are small invertebrates whose bodies have a hard outer casing. They have six legs and feelers called antennae. Many have wings.

CAN YOU FIND?
1. eggs
2. a caterpillar
3. a chrysalis
4. a butterfly

▼ Leaf-cutter ants carry leaves across the floors of tropical forests. They chew the leaves into a pulp, and they eat a fungus that grows on the pulp.

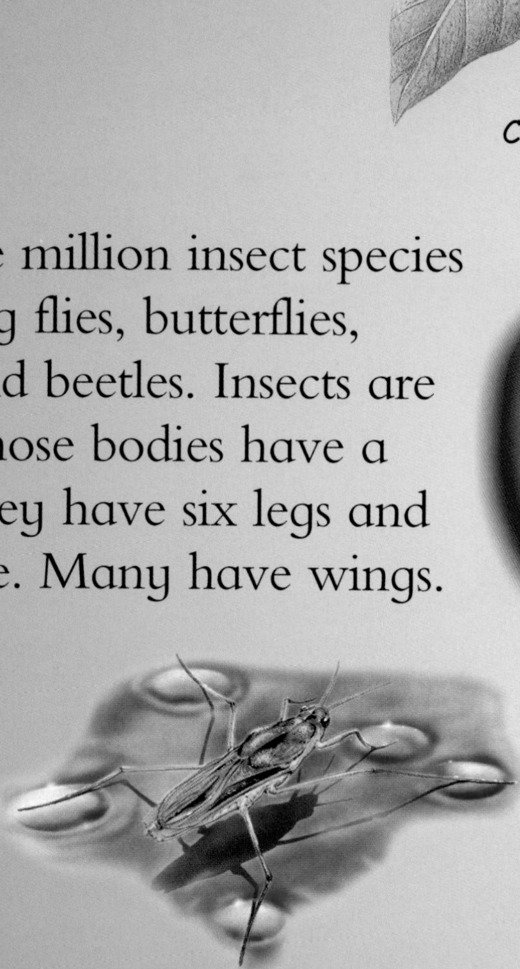

◀ The pond skater walks across the filmy surface of ponds, searching for other insects to eat.

Butterfly
emerging

▲ The monarch butterfly
lays eggs on the milkweed
plant. The caterpillar hatches
and eats the leaves. It turns
into a chrysalis, which then
changes into a butterfly.

Wasp nests

Some wasps chew tiny pieces
of wood and mix it with saliva
to make a beautiful paper nest.
The queen wasp lays her eggs
in the nest. The wasps defend
the nest fiercely and can
deliver a very painful sting.

CREATIVE CORNER

Making a butterfly mobile

Fold four sheets of 8$\frac{1}{2}$ x 11-inch
paper in half and then draw butterfly
shapes on each. Cut out both sides of the
fold as shown. Color in wing patterns
and body shapes. Make a mobile using
three plastic drinking straws and string.
Tie on the butterflies and hang the
mobile from the ceiling.

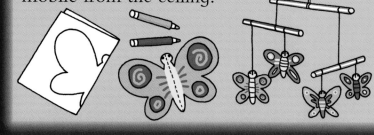

INTERNET LINKS: www.ivyhall.district96.k12.il.us/4TH/KKHP/1INSECTS/bugmenu.html

Spiders

Spiders belong to a group of eight-legged invertebrates called arachnids. Spiders may be tiny, big, or hairy. Millions of spiders may be found in just one grassy field. Spiders can produce silk, which they use to swing through the air, protect their eggs, and capture the insects that they eat.

► This European garden spider has caught a fly in its strong, sticky, silken web. Spiders eat a huge number of insects.

Black widow
spider, U.S.

Wandering
spider, Brazil

▲ Spiders have fangs for killing their prey. Most spiders are harmless to humans, but these two are deadly.

CREATIVE CORNER

Spider web

Twist three pipe cleaners to make the six "spokes" of the spider web. Then tie one end of a piece of thread to a spoke near the center. Move in an outward spiral, looping the thread around each spoke. When the web is complete, cut the thread and tie a knot. Draw, color, and cut out a spider on a piece of paper and stick it in the middle of the web.

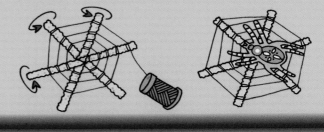

Scorpions

Scorpions are arachnids that live in hot countries and are often found in deserts. They have big pincers and arching tails with venomous stingers. They eat mostly insects and spiders.

▼ A scorpion carries her young on her back. After around 12 days, they are ready to take care of themselves.

WHY DO SCORPIONS DANCE?
Before scorpions mate, they perform a courtship dance. During this dance, they wave their pincers and tails in the air.

The tale of Arachne
The ancient Greeks told a tale about a proud woman named Arachne. When she challenged the goddess Athena to a weaving contest, the goddess became very angry. She turned Arachne and her descendants into spiders.

▶ If a scorpion is threatened, it can inject a deadly venom into the animal that has threatened it. It does this through the curved spine at the end of its tail.

73

Fish

Fish are animals that swim in rivers, lakes, and oceans. They have bodies that are covered in scales. Some species may be tiny, while others are giants up to 50 ft. (15m) long. Many fish eat insects or water creatures, including other fish. Some feed on plankton, which are tiny creatures and plants that drift in oceans.

HOW MANY FISH ARE THERE?
Around 27,700 species of fish live in the oceans, and around 2,300 species live in streams, rivers, and lakes.

Tail fin

Dorsal fin

Gills

Anal fin

Pectoral fin

Pelvic fin

Fish bodies

Fish are vertebrates. They use their tails and fins to help them swim and stay balanced in the water. Most fish take in the oxygen that they need by passing water through the gills behind their heads.

◄ The great white shark is one of the most feared animals in the ocean. It has rows of pointed teeth. It usually eats seals and sea lions, but occasionally it will attack humans.

◄ Corals are small creatures that live in warm oceans. As they die, their chalky remains build up into banks called coral reefs. All types of fish make their homes in reefs.

A fish that saved the world

Hindus tell how at the dawn of this age a man named Manu saved a tiny fish that he had found in a river. The fish, Matsya, grew bigger and bigger, for it was really the god Vishnu. Manu first put Matsya in a bowl, then in a tank, then in a lake, and finally in the ocean. Matsya warned Manu that a great flood was on the way. He told Manu to build a boat and fill it with the seeds of all living things. The boat was towed to a high mountain, where it survived the great flood.

Amphibians

Amphibians are animals that live partly in the water and partly on land. They include frogs, toads, newts, and salamanders. Most species lay their eggs in the water. The young breathe underwater through gills, but they may later develop lungs to breathe air.

Axolotl
This amphibian lives in only two lakes in Mexico. Its feathery gills extend outside its body. Axolotls generally stay in this stage of development, without ever growing into land animals.

◀ Male midwife toads carry strings of eggs around on their back legs. After three weeks, they enter the water, where the eggs hatch.

The frog prince
The way in which frogs change shape inspired many fairy tales. One tells of a princess who is helped by an ugly frog. She does not realize that he is really a handsome prince who has been turned into a frog by a wicked fairy. The spell is broken only when she kisses him.

▼ The common frog lives in marshes and other damp areas. It lays its eggs, or spawn, in ponds.

Frog spawn

Tadpole

Smooth newt

Fire salamander

▲ Newts and salamanders have long bodies and keep their tails as adults. They eat small creatures such as worms and slugs.

CREATIVE CORNER

Swimming like a frog

The rear legs of frogs are very powerful. Can you swim frog style? The next time you go swimming, have a competition to see who can go the longest distance with only three froggy leg kicks.

▲ Tree frogs live in rainforests. They have disk-shaped suckers on their toes that help them climb up trees to hunt insects. They return to ponds to lay their eggs.

Tadpole developing legs

Frog

Reptiles

Reptiles include snakes, lizards, alligators, crocodiles, tortoises, turtles, and terrapins. They are egg-laying vertebrates whose bodies are protected by scales or horny plates. Reptiles are cold-blooded creatures, so they are unable to create their own body warmth. This is why they bask, lying in the warm sunshine to raise their temperature. Snakes and some lizards have no legs.

WHY DO SNAKES FLICK THEIR TONGUES?
Snakes have forked tongues with special sensors that help them "taste" the air and pick up the scent of their prey.

▲ The giant tortoises that live on the Galápagos Islands can grow up to 5 ft. (1.5m) long and weigh more than 298 lbs. (135kg). They eat grass, leaves, and the fruit of the cactus.

▲ Green turtles come ashore to lay their eggs, which they bury in the sand. Weeks later, the babies hatch and race to the safety of the ocean.

Changing color

Chameleons live mostly in Africa. They are lizards with long tongues and swiveling eyes. Their bodies can change color with changes in light or temperature or when they are afraid or angry.

Crocodile

Alligator

▲ Wagler's pit viper is a snake that lives in Southeast Asia. It can survive for weeks on only one meal, swallowing rats, birds, or lizards whole.

▲ Spot the difference between the crocodile and the alligator. The fourth tooth on the crocodile's lower jaw sticks up outside its snout. Both reptiles are large and powerful hunters.

INTERNET LINKS: www.amonline.net.au/wild_kids/reptiles/crocodile.htm • http://home.cfl.rr.com/gatorhole/

◀ Swallows spend the winter in the far south, but each summer they fly to North America, northern Europe, and Asia in order to breed. Long animal journeys are called migrations.

Birds

Birds are found almost everywhere in the world, from tropical forests to the icy coasts of Antarctica. Birds are egg-laying vertebrates whose bodies are covered in feathers. Most birds are able to fly, but some are flightless.

The falcon god

Ancient peoples revered birds because they could fly. Birds were sometimes thought to be spirits or the messengers of the gods. In ancient Egypt, the god Horus was the protector of the pharaoh, the Egyptian king. Horus was often pictured with the head of a falcon, which is a bird of prey.

WHY DO BIRDS HAVE FEATHERS?

Feathers keep birds warm and also make it possible for them to fly. Underneath the outer feathers are small, fluffy feathers called down.

▶ Sea birds, such as gannets, eat fish and shellfish. They can paddle, swim, and dive as well as fly. Many sea birds nest on the ledges of steep cliffs in large groups called colonies.

Ostrich

Emu

Rhea

Kiwi

▶ These birds are all flightless. They walk or run, but cannot use their wings. Ostriches live in Africa, emus in Australia, rheas in South America, and kiwis in New Zealand.

CREATIVE CORNER

Winter food for wild birds

Take half a coconut shell or an empty plastic container. Then ask an adult to melt some shortening or butter in a pan. Mix in seeds, unsalted nuts, oats, cereal, bacon rinds, or cheese. Pour this mixture into the upturned shell or container and leave it to set. Turn the container upside down and hang it up outside, well away from cats.

A frightened
rabbit runs as a golden
eagle closes in for the kill.
This bird of prey has a hooked
beak and very sharp talons.

What is a mammal?

Cats, dogs, elephants, monkeys, rabbits, whales, and humans are all mammals. Mammals are warm-blooded vertebrates that breathe air. They feed their babies on mothers' milk. Mammals are the most intelligent animals on Earth.

▲ Mice can have babies several times each year. They are gnawing mammals, or rodents, and live in most parts of the world.

▲ A baby African elephant can be 3 ft. (1m) tall and weigh up to 200 lbs. (90kg). An adult may grow to 10.5 ft. (3.3m) and weigh five tons.

◄ The platypus is an unusual mammal because it lays eggs. It lives on Australian riverbanks. It has claws and webbed feet and a bill shaped like a duck's.

Warm fur

A mother harp seal feeds her white pup on thick, rich, creamy milk. Seals' bodies have a layer of fatty blubber and a hairy fur coat that keeps them warm in cold seas and on the frozen ice.

▲ A baby kangaroo is called a joey. It is raised inside a pouch on the front of its mother's body. Pouched animals are called marsupials.

Brer Rabbit

Animal stories that teach us about the way that humans behave are called fables. African–American folktales tell of Brer (Brother) Rabbit, a saucy trickster who always outwits his rival, the rascal Brer Fox.

▲ A female pig is called a sow. A male pig is called a boar. This sow has given birth to a litter of 14 piglets. They are all fighting to drink her milk.

Meat-eating mammals

Mammals that eat meat, including big cats, wild dogs, bears, and seals, are called carnivores. Some carnivores hunt and kill live prey such as fish, birds, deer, or rabbits. Others feed mostly on dead animals, or carrion.

▲ A giant anteater in South America uses its claws to break up a termites' nest. It has a long, sticky tongue to catch and eat the insects.

▲ The American black bear catches salmon, birds, mice and other small mammals, and insects. It also likes to feed on berries and nuts.

? WHAT IS A FOOD CHAIN?

Animals eat other animals or plants in order to stay alive. A fox eats a bird. A bird eats a snail. A snail eats a leaf. This sequence is called a food chain.

▲ Shrews are insect eaters. They are tiny creatures with pointed noses. To stay alive, they must eat their own weight in food each day.

▼ Lionesses chase a small antelope on the grassy plains of Africa. Lions are powerful and fierce hunters. They live in groups called prides.

How the leopard got its spots

In the *Just-So Stories*, written in 1902, an English writer named Rudyard Kipling tells the funny story about how the African animals got their stripes and spots. He claims that the five-spot patterns on a leopard's coat are the marks of fingerprints from the hand of a hunter.

Hyenas

Packs of hyenas live in Africa and Asia. They can hunt for themselves but mostly live on dead animals, or carrion. They scavenge the scraps and bones when lions or other creatures make a kill.

INTERNET LINKS: http://nationalzoo.si.edu/Animals/GreatCats/catskids.cfm

Plant-eating mammals

Animals that can digest plants such as grass or leaves are called herbivores. They include mammals such as horses, cows, goats, deer, antelope, and camels. Animals that get all of their energy from plants need to graze most of the time.

▼ The African elephant eats grasses, leaves, fruit, and branches. It uses its trunk to smell, carry food or water to its mouth, spray water, and lift objects.

▲ Bison, or buffalo, live on prairies, the grasslands of North America. Here, two males charge at each other to win a female.

VOCABULARY

graze
To feed on grasses and herbs.

dromedary
An African or Arabian camel that has a single hump. The rare Bactrian camel from Asia has two humps.

► The giraffe eats various twigs and leaves. Its long neck allows it to feed on high branches that smaller animals cannot reach. Its mouth is protected from sharp thorns.

► The Arabian camel, or dromedary, lives in hot deserts, eating any leaves and bushes that it can find. It can travel for long distances without water. Its hump is a store of fat that the camel converts into food.

WHY DO ELEPHANTS HAVE TUSKS?

Tusks are special teeth. They can be used for digging, tearing bark from trees, and attacking enemies.

CREATIVE CORNER

Nature detective
Watch out for signs of different animals feeding in parks and woods. Acorns, nuts, and pinecones may have been gnawed by squirrels. Bark may have been stripped from trees by deer. Short grass may have been grazed by cattle, sheep, or rabbits.

Marsupials

Marsupials are a group of animals found in Australia and the Americas. They include kangaroos, Tasmanian devils, wallabies, bandicoots, koalas, wombats, Australian possums, and American opossums. When a marsupial baby is still tiny, it climbs inside its mother's pouch and grows there.

▲ There are more than 60 species of possums living in Australia and on the islands of New Guinea and Sulawesi (Indonesia). These marsupials are tree creatures that come out at night.

WHO PLAYS POSSUM?

"Playing possum" means pretending to be dead. Opossums in North America get limp when they are in danger so that attackers leave them alone.

▼ Koalas are marsupials that look like small bears. After a koala leaves the pouch, it may be carried on its mother's back. Koalas feed on eucalyptus leaves.

How Opossum got a pouch

An old Native American tale tells how Big Bat kidnapped Opossum's babies. Terrapin rescued them and made a special pouch for Opossum to keep her babies inside so that nobody could ever steal them again.

Bats

There are more than 1,000 species of bats in the world. Bats are flying mammals that come out to feed at dusk. Most bats eat insects, but some eat fruit, nectar, or fish. A few suck blood from birds or cattle. By day, bats roost in caves, trees, or buildings.

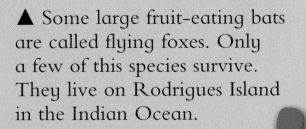

▲ Some large fruit-eating bats are called flying foxes. Only a few of this species survive. They live on Rodrigues Island in the Indian Ocean.

▲ Thousands of Mediterranean horseshoe bats may roost in the same cave. Bats usually hang upside down with their claws hooked onto a ledge.

How bats find their prey

Bats give out a high-pitched sound as they fly. If the sound meets another object, such as a moth, an echo bounces back to the bat. This helps them find prey in the dark.

INTERNET LINKS: www.iwrc-online.org/kids/Facts/Mammals/marsupials.htm

Ocean mammals

The world's oceans are full of fish and other tasty sea creatures. Many mammals have taken to living in or around oceans in order to catch them. They include seals, sea lions, walrus, whales, dolphins and porpoises, manatees, and polar bears.

Jonah and the whale

During a storm at sea, Jonah was thrown overboard and swallowed by a whale. He lived inside the whale for three days before being spat out onto dry land.

▼ Walrus live in the far northern waters of the world. They are big, heavy mammals. Walrus have tusks that are up to 3 ft. (1m) long. They use their tusks to scrape clams from the ocean floor.

▼ Harp seals are deep-sea divers that live in cold, northern oceans. They hunt Arctic cod. Like all mammals, they must come to the surface to breathe air.

CAN YOU FIND?
1. tusks
2. teeth
3. flippers
4. tails
5. cubs

Right whale,
a filter feeder

▲ Polar bears live in the Arctic. They cross the ice to hunt seals, fish, and birds. They are very strong swimmers.

▶ Whales and ocean dolphins such as the killer whale look like huge fish, but they are mammals. Some whales filter tiny creatures from the ocean as they swim along. Others have sharp teeth for attacking fish or seals.

Killer whale,
a dolphin with teeth

INTERNET LINKS: www.whalewatch.com/kids/

Apes and monkeys

Monkeys and apes are the closest relatives of human beings. We all belong to an intelligent group of mammals called primates. Apes have no tails and sometimes walk upright. Monkeys usually live in trees and can swing through the branches using their long arms and tails.

▼ Gorillas are big apes. They have powerful bodies but are really gentle giants. They live in the mountains and forests of Africa, where they eat fruit, leaves, bark, and roots.

WHAT DOES ORANGUTAN MEAN?

In the Malay language, the word *orangutan* means "man of the jungle."

Naughty monkey

One of the most famous old Chinese books is called *The Journey to the West*. Its hero is a saucy animal named Monkey. Monkey plays naughty tricks, fights monsters and dragons, performs acrobatics, and travels from China to India.

▼ Orangutans are apes that live in Southeast Asia. They build nests in the treetops and eat fruit, birds' eggs, and honeycombs. Sadly, many of their forests are being cut down.

▲ Nine species of howler monkeys live in the rainforests of Central and South America. Their tails help them cling to branches. Howlers are large monkeys and can roar very loudly.

Using tools

A chimpanzee, watched by its baby, uses a stick to poke termites out of a mound. This intelligent ape has learned to use tools in its search for food. Chimpanzees live in large groups in African forests.

INTERNET LINKS: www.nationalgeographic.com/kids/creature_feature/0102/orangutans.html

Animals in danger

The world is filling with more and more people. They build new towns and roads. They cut down forests and drain swamps where animals live. Land, water, and air are poisoned. Many animals find it hard to survive these changes. Some are even in danger of becoming extinct.

▲ Animals that have very little land to live on are at risk. The Komodo dragon is the world's biggest lizard. It lives on only a few tiny islands in Indonesia.

▲ Queen Alexandra's birdwing is the world's biggest butterfly. It is found in only one forest area in Papua New Guinea. Parts of this are being cut down.

Rhinos and unicorns

Five species of rhinoceros live in Asia and Africa. All are in danger of dying out because they are hunted for their horns. In the Middle Ages, the rhino's strange horn inspired all kinds of tales about unicorns.

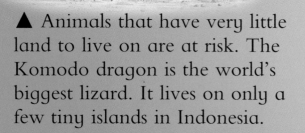

VOCABULARY

conservation
Protecting animals and looking after where they live.

habitat
The type of land in which an animal naturally lives such as a forest or desert.

▶ The beautiful quetzal lives in Central America. For years, it was hunted for its feathers. Now the forests where it lives are being cleared by poor farmers in order to grow crops.

◀ Bengal tigers live in India. They are protected animals, but hunters still kill them. They are also losing their habitat. There may be only around 4,500 left in the wild.

◀ The giant panda is very rare. It lives in the misty bamboo forests of China. These are being cut back as villages grow. The panda is an international symbol of animal conservation.

CREATIVE CORNER

Designing a poster

Make a colorful poster to let people know about an animal or a habitat that is under threat. It might show a tiger or a panda or maybe animals from a local forest that is due to be cut down.

Now you know!

▲ Butterflies are insects. They have wings and six legs.

▲ Spiders have eight legs. Their bodies can produce silky thread to make webs.

▲ Swallows migrate every year. They fly thousands of miles from one continent to another.

▲ Frogs are amphibians. They spend their lives in water and on land.

▲ Snails are mollusks. They have soft bodies that are protected by the hard shells on their backs.

▲ Snakes are reptiles. They bask in the sun to get warm.

▲ Most fish can breathe underwater. They do this by using gills, which are openings on the sides of their heads.

◀ A baby kangaroo is called a joey. When it is first born, it climbs up inside its mother's pouch.

Dinosaurs

What were dinosaurs? When did they live?
The prehistoric world is a fascinating subject.
Experts are gradually putting together a good
picture of what our world was like millions of
years ago when dinosaurs roamed Earth.

What are dinosaurs?

Dinosaurs were reptiles that lived on Earth long before humans ever appeared. These reptiles dominated life on land for more than 150 million years before dying out around 65 million years ago. There were many different types of dinosaurs. They lived during different periods of time and on every continent of the world.

◀ Like other fossils, those of dinosaurs are often found in cliffs or rock faces, where the surface of the rock has worn away to expose the layers beneath.

▲ When footprints or other marks left by dinosaurs are preserved as fossils, they are called trace fossils. These can tell us about dinosaur behavior.

▲ When a dinosaur died, its soft parts rotted away. Some dinosaur bones sank into mud and, over thousands of years, turned into rock.

Oviraptor

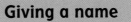
Triceratops

North America

Mongolia

Patagonia

Ouranosaurus

Argentinosaurus

Giving a name

The word *dinosaur* means "terrible lizard." It was first given to these ancient creatures in 1842 by an English paleontologist, or fossil expert, named Richard Owen. He wanted the name to reflect the enormous size of many of the large dinosaurs.

▲ Dinosaur fossils have been found all over the world. There have been recent large finds in the areas marked on the map. This means that experts now know important information about the dinosaurs found there.

◄ Fossils are not usually complete skeletons. Sometimes only a few bones are found, and scientists have to guess what the rest of the animal might have looked like.

▲ Millions of years later, scientists find the fossil skeleton. They carefully dig it out from the ground and try to figure out what the animal looked like when it was alive.

▲ In order to show people what dinosaurs looked like, many museums reconstruct entire skeletons. The leg bones of this plant eater give an idea of how gigantic the entire animal would have been.

Dinosaur timeline

The time when the dinosaurs lived is called the Mesozoic era. It was the time between two major events in which many animals became extinct, or died out. During the Mesozoic era, Earth was very warm, which helped new animal types develop.

Dinosaur timeline

Triassic

Jurassic

Cretaceous

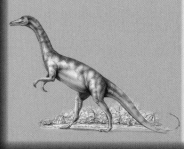

245 million years ago

208 million years ago

144 million years ago

Be there dragons?
Dragons feature in the folklore of many countries, often as symbols of power. They were probably made up by early people to explain the large fossil bones of dinosaurs that they found.

Triassic

▼ The early dinosaurs in the Triassic were small. However, in the Late Triassic there were some large plant eaters such as *Plateosaurus*.

Early dinosaurs
Coelophysis was a small dinosaur with hollow bones. It was a quick-moving hunter and meat eater that lived in the Late Triassic. It is one of the earliest known dinosaurs.

urassic

▼ In the Late Jurassic, *Allosaurus* was the largest meat-eating dinosaur in North America. The first birds and modern mammals also developed during this period.

Insect eaters
Compsognathus (above) was a small chicken-size dinosaur that lived in Europe in the Late Jurassic. It probably ate insects and small lizards.

Cretaceous

▼ New groups of dinosaurs appeared in the Cretaceous. *Struthiomimus* ("ostrich mimic") had long legs for running away.

Ready for attack
Tyrannosaurs lived at this time, and many plant eaters had to defend themselves from attacks. Ankylosaurs (below) could not run easily, so they relied on their well-armored bodies, with their bony plates or spikes.

INTERNET LINKS: www.cotf.edu/ete/modules/msese/dinosaurflr/meet.html

Types of dinosaurs

Around 300 types of dinosaurs lived in many different parts of the world from 230 million years ago until they died out 65 million years ago. Dinosaurs were reptiles, and they were all shapes and sizes. Today's reptiles include lizards, snakes, crocodiles, and tortoises. Like most other reptiles, dinosaurs lived on land and laid eggs.

► Some dinosaurs were as tall as houses, while some were as small as chickens. The carnivores (meat eaters) among them would either hunt their prey or eat dead animals that they found. Other dinosaurs were herbivores (plant eaters) that ate trees and other plants.

CAN YOU FIND?
1. scales
2. spines
3. horns
4. a tail
5. jaws
6. teeth

Apatosaurus
(plant eater)

Spinosaurus
(meat eater)

Styracosaurus
(plant eater)

Panoplosaurus
(plant eater)

Oviraptor
(meat eater)

Stygimoloc
(plant eate

VOCABULARY

reptile

A cold-blooded, scaly, four-legged animal that lays its eggs on land.

skeleton

The framework of bones that holds up the body of an animal.

Saurischian *Tyrannosaurus* skeleton

Ornithischian *Stegosaurus* skeleton

▲ Scientists divide dinosaurs into two main groups. The saurischians, "lizard-hipped dinosaurs" (top), have hips similar to modern-day lizards. The ornithischians, "bird-hipped dinosaurs" (above), have hips similar to modern-day birds.

Modern-day dinosaurs?

The thorny devil lizard lives in Australia today. It has cone-shaped spines all over its body to protect it from predators. There are similar spines on some of the dinosaurs on this page.

Iguanodon
(plant eater)

Kentrosaurus
(plant eater)

Finding fossils

When the fossil of a dinosaur is found, a team of experts and scientists get together. They excavate it, or dig it out of the ground, very carefully. The fossilized parts of a skeleton are taken away for scientists to examine.

▶ When the fossil is first uncovered, an artist draws an exact picture of it. This helps people put the skeleton together again later in a museum.

? WHERE ARE FOSSILS FOUND?
Fossils are usually found where sun, rain, or wind wear away the surrounding rock and expose them.

◀ Photographs of each section of the fossil are taken to record the exact position of the bones.

◄ Fossils are very delicate. The surrounding soil must be removed carefully so that they are not damaged. This person is using a soft brush to gently sweep away the soil from the bones.

◄ Once the bones are removed from the ground, they are wrapped very carefully in plaster of Paris to protect them while they are loaded into a truck and transported, usually over very bumpy ground.

CAN YOU FIND?
1. a camera
2. tailbones
3. a hammer
4. skull bones
5. the spine
6. an artist

CREATIVE CORNER

Making a fossil of a twig
Press a twig into a piece of modeling clay and remove it. Brush a little cooking oil onto the clay and then mix some plaster of Paris and pour it into the shape of the twig. When the plaster is dry, gently remove the clay from your fossil twig.

INTERNET LINKS: www.bbc.co.uk/sn/prehistoric_life/dinosaurs/making_fossils/

Meat-eating dinosaurs

The meat-eating dinosaurs, the carnosaurs, were ferocious. They used their sharp teeth and claws to catch their prey. Some, such as *Avimimus*, were fast runners and chased after their prey. Others, such as *Allosaurus*, probably hunted by hiding until a prey animal came close.

A meaty diet

When a dinosaur or other animal is described as a carnivore, it simply means that it eats the flesh of other animals. Some carnivorous dinosaurs hunted and killed prey for themselves. Some fed on prey killed by other predators or animals that had died natural deaths. Many dinosaurs survived on whatever was available. They ate other dinosaurs, fish, and the eggs of birds and other dinosaurs.

◀ *Tyrannosaurus* had thick, curved teeth. We know that its prey included the horned dinosaur *Triceratops* because the sawlike edges at the back and front left distinctive marks on the bones.

▶ The tyrannosaurs, or "tyrant lizards," were among the largest meat eaters. This one is attacking a *Corythosaurus*, or "helmet lizard."

Tyrannosaurus

Ankylosaurus

Corythosaurus

◀ Meat-eating dinosaurs came in all shapes and sizes. Each of them was specially adapted for catching and eating prey. Most, like carnivores today, had strong jaws, sharp teeth, and claws.

7

4

5

6

2

3

1

1. *Avimimus* **2.** *Oviraptor* **3.** *Struthiomimus*
4. *Dilophosaurus* **5.** *Allosaurus*
6. *Troodon* **7.** *Tyrannosaurus*

VOCABULARY

prey
An animal that other, often larger, animals hunt and eat.

predator
An animal that hunts and eats other animals as prey.

WHAT WERE HORNS FOR?
Horns may have helped protect plant eaters, like this *Triceratops* (below), from predators.

Ornithomimus

CREATIVE CORNER

Making a carnosaur tooth
Shape a carnosaur tooth out of bakeable modeling clay, using the tooth on page 106 as a model. Ask an adult to bake the clay for you. Then paint it to look just like a real carnosaur tooth!

Triceratops

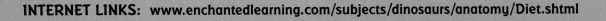

Dinosaur weapons

Many dinosaurs were equipped with natural weapons—their teeth, horns, and claws. Some used these body parts to attack other animals while hunting for food or fighting for territory. Some used them only to defend themselves or their young. Many dinosaurs relied on them for both attack and defense.

? HOW DID THEY HUNT?

There is evidence that some dinosaurs, such as *Deinonychus*, hunted in packs. Others, such as *Tyrannosaurus*, may have hunted alone.

▶ Some dinosaurs, like these *Oviraptors*, ate the eggs of other dinosaurs when they could find them. Long claws were useful for hooking eggs out of nests.

CAN YOU FIND?

1. a thumb claw
2. sickle-shaped claws
3. a long snout
4. an egg stealer
5. prey
6. predators

◀ *Deinonychus* probably hunted in packs. Its name means "terrible claw," after its ferocious claws on both front and rear limbs, including a huge, sicklelike claw on its second toe.

▲ *Allosaurus* was one of the most successful predators. Its sharp, pointed teeth and strong jaws were perfectly suited for tearing meat and crushing bones.

◀ *Baryonyx* may have used its large thumb claws to hook fish out of the water and then catch in its long snout.

Deadly claws

The claws on *Deinonychus*'s second toes were curved and turned up. They were weapons of pure destruction. Experts are not sure whether the dinosaur would have used them for stabbing or slashing prey.

CREATIVE CORNER

A moving dinosaur jaw

Cut two long strips of construction paper and cut out tooth shapes. Now punch holes into both ends of the strips. Push a pencil through, bending the paper. Wind rubber bands around the pencil to keep the paper in place.

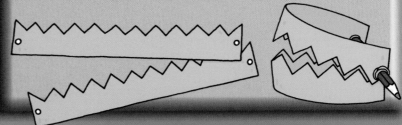

INTERNET LINKS: www.enchantedlearning.com/subjects/dinosaurs/anatomy/Defense.shtml

Fiercest of all

The tyrannosaurs were the fiercest of all the predators. They were also among the largest known meat-eating land animals of all time. Some scientists believe that smaller tyrannosaurs could run and catch plant eaters larger than themselves.

▶ *Tyrannosaurus rex* stood more than 26 ft. (8m) tall. It ate dead dinosaurs that it found and followed herds of plant eaters, attacking any old, sick, or young animals that became separated from the pack.

WHAT DID THEY LOOK LIKE?
We do not know what color dinosaurs were, but experts usually assume that they blended into their natural habitats.

Basking lizard
Modern reptiles, such as this lizard, are cold-blooded. They need to bask in the sun to stay warm. For a long time, scientists believed that dinosaurs were cold-blooded. Now they think that some were warm-blooded—able to generate their own heat, like modern birds and mammals.

► The family of tyrannosaurs belonged to a group of dinosaurs called theropods. Theropods walked on two feet and had three toes on each foot.

Allosaurus

Dilophosaurus

Albertosaurus

► Little is known about dinosaur skin because it is not usually preserved. This fossil of a *Carnotaurus* shows that it had scaly skin, so it is possible that *Tyrannosaurus* also had scales like this.

▲ A *Tyrannosaurus*'s skull was half as long as its body. It must have had very strong neck muscles to support the weight. Its teeth were curved and very sharp. It used them to tear chunks of meat to eat.

CREATIVE CORNER

Dinosaur-hunting game

Each player has two counters. The first player moves one of his counters to the empty central spot. Taking turns, the players continue to move one counter at a time to an empty spot, until one player can no longer move.

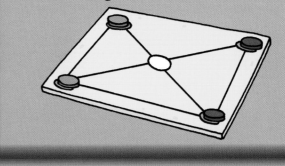

INTERNET LINKS: www.nhm.ac.uk/nature-online/life/dinosaurs-other-extinct-creatures/trex-quiz/

Plant-eating dinosaurs

The herbivores, or plant-eating dinosaurs, were often much larger than the carnivores, or meat-eating dinosaurs. However, they were usually slower, which meant that the meat eaters could hunt them. Many plant eaters had long necks so that they could reach up to the leaves on tall plants and trees.

WHY DID THEY EAT PLANTS?

Plants get energy from the sun and store it. Plant-eating dinosaurs ate the plants to give themselves energy.

▼ The largest dinosaurs were the plant eaters. If it stood on its hind legs, this *Barosaurus* could lift its enormous head up almost 50 ft. (15m) into the air to feed on treetops.

Pisanosaurus:
Late Triassic

Echinodon: Late Triassic
to Early Cretaceous

Lesothosaurus:
Late Triassic to
Early Jurassic

▲ There were many different species in the family of ornithischians, or "bird-hipped dinosaurs." They were all herbivores.

VOCABULARY

species
A group of animals that can breed with each other, but not with other species.

ginkgo
A medium-size tree that developed around 270 million years ago.

Plants the dinosaurs ate
When dinosaurs lived on Earth, the plants were very different from today's plants. Early plants were ferns (like this horsetail), ginkgos, and conifers. Flowering plants and seeds did not develop until the Cretaceous period.

▲ *Edmontosaurus* was a large plant-eating dinosaur that lived during the Late Cretaceous. It was around 43 ft. (13m) long. Its skull (above) shows that it had many small teeth, used for grinding up plants.

INTERNET LINKS: www.enchantedlearning.com/subjects/dinosaurs/plants/

Dinosaur giants

Among the first plant–eating dinosaurs and the first land animals that were tall enough to feed on trees were the prosauropods such as *Plateosaurus*. Prosauropods lived all over the world, and there were more of them than any other large land animal. They were replaced by the sauropods, the true giants of the dinosaur world.

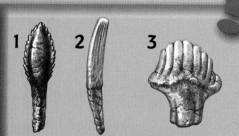

Dinosaur teeth

Plateosaurus's sharp, leaflike teeth (1) and *Diplodocus*'s pencil-shaped teeth (2) would have been good for stripping plants. *Stegosaurus*'s blunt, ridged teeth (3) could nip off leaves and probably chew them, too.

▼ *Seismosaurus* was a diplodocid. This family of dinosaurs had very long necks and tails. A *Seismosaurus* reached up to 36 ft. (11m) tall.

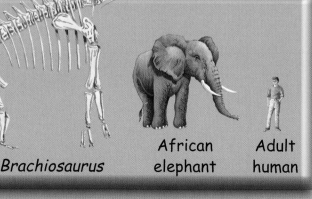

Brachiosaurus   African elephant   Adult human

▲ *Supersaurus* may have been up to 115 ft. (35m) long. Its name means "super lizard," and this dinosaur was probably the largest member of the diplodocid family.

Grinding up food

The plant-eating sauropods, such as *Apatosaurus* and *Brachiosaurus*, did not really need to chew their food. They swallowed stones to help grind up their food inside their bodies. These stones are called gastroliths. Some modern birds, crocodiles, and seals also use gastroliths.

Gastroliths

HOW HEAVY WERE THEY?

The largest dinosaur may have weighed up to 100 tons—or almost as much as a modern blue whale.

◀ *Brachiosaurus*'s name means "arm lizard" because its forelegs, or "arms," were longer than its rear legs. It was around 82 ft. (25m) long and for many years was the longest dinosaur that had been discovered.

INTERNET LINKS: http://members.aol.com/DinoPixels/sauro_gallery.html

Self-defense

Like modern animals, dinosaurs had to defend themselves. Many of them were preyed on by meat-eating dinosaurs. The adults needed to protect their young from attacks, and males sometimes would have fought over territory or females.

▲ Pachycephalosaurs had thickened bones on the tops of their skulls. They probably fought one another by butting heads.

VOCABULARY

hide
The pelt or skin of a larger animal.

territory
An area in which an animal lives and protects from others of its type.

Bony plate on back

Spike on tail

▶ The bony plates on *Stegosaurus*'s back look tough, but they were made of thin bone and probably did not protect the animal well. However, *Stegosaurus* had a very thick hide and a ferociously spiked tail that it could swing at an attacker.

Protective tails

Ankylosaurus (1) had a lump of thickened bone on the end of its tail, like a club. *Stegosaurus*'s (2) bony spikes were covered in horn. Some experts believe that *Diplodocus* (3) used its long, whiplike tail in self-defense.

1

2

3

▶ The name *Triceratops* means "three-horned face." This plant eater may have used its horns in self-defense, but experts now believe that it used them mostly for display, a lot like modern reindeer.

CREATIVE CORNER

Matching animals

Some of today's animals have defensive weapons that are similar to those of dinosaurs. See if you can find and copy pictures of modern animals with similar modes of defense such as horns, tusks, or scales.

INTERNET LINKS: www.amnh.org/exhibitions/dinosaurs/display/

Dinosaur babies

Dinosaurs reproduced by laying eggs. The eggs protected the young dinosaurs inside and provided them with food while they grew. It is difficult to say whether dinosaurs were caring parents, but there is evidence that some looked after their eggs and young.

◀ *Oviraptors* laid their eggs and then covered them with sand. By sitting on top, the parents' body heat would have kept the eggs warm at night.

Egg stealer?

The first *Oviraptor* discovered was sitting on top of a nest of eggs. The scientists thought that it had been killed trying to steal another dinosaur's eggs—its name means "egg thief." In fact, it had probably died trying to protect its own eggs, not stealing those of other dinosaurs.

VOCABULARY

reproduce
To produce babies or young animals.

embryo
The form of a partly grown baby animal, like those found in eggs before they are hatched.

WHAT SHAPE WERE THE EGGS?

Dinosaur eggs were either round or oval, like footballs or basketballs. They also had hard, brittle shells.

◀ *Maiasaura*'s name means "good mother lizard." Many *Maiasaura* nests have been found with the remains of adults, young, embryos, and broken eggshells. This suggests that the adults cared for their eggs and young.

▲ Fossilized footprints suggest that *Apatosaurus* traveled in herds. The young were kept in the middle of the group to protect them from predators.

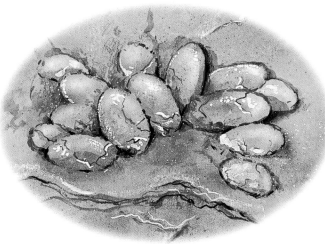

▲ Some dinosaurs made nests, like the fossilized one shown here, found in China. Others laid their eggs in a row, as if they laid them while they were walking along.

INTERNET LINKS: www.facts.com/gdns-0000100.htm • http://search.eb.com/dinosaurs/dinosaurs/BO.html

Reptiles of the oceans

The word *dinosaur* is sometimes incorrectly used for other prehistoric creatures such as pterosaurs and various types of marine, or ocean-living, reptiles. These animals were related to dinosaurs but evolved as separate groups.

▶ Plesiosaurs were a large group of marine reptiles. There were two types of plesiosaurs. One type, such as *Elasmosaurus*, had long necks and large bodies. The other, such as *Kronosaurus*, had short necks, large heads, and strong jaws.

▲ *Archelon*'s name means "ancient turtle." The largest turtle that ever lived, it was 13 ft. (4m) long and 16 ft. (5m) wide from flipper to flipper.

Kronosaurus

The Loch Ness monster

In 1933, someone spotted what he or she thought was a large animal in Loch Ness, a lake in Scotland. The "Loch Ness monster" is often said to look like a plesiosaur. But it is highly unlikely that an animal of this size would have gone unseen until the 1900s.

Mosasaurus

CAN YOU FIND?

1. flippers
2. a long neck
3. sharp teeth
4. a long snout
5. a body covered with a shell
6. scales

Elasmosaurus

▲ *Ichthyosaurus,* or "fish lizard," was called this because of its body shape. Some fossils have been found with the bones of baby ichthyosaurs inside, so experts believe that they gave birth to live young, rather than laying eggs.

Ichthyosaurus

Teleosaurus

Food in prehistoric oceans

Different marine reptiles fed on different sea creatures and plants. The marine lizard *Mosasaurus* ate fish and turtles and prized ammonites out of their shells. The crocodile-shaped *Teleosaurus* had long jaws that were good for catching fish and squids. Dolphinlike *Ichthyosaurus* ate fish, squids, and shellfish that it crushed in its jaws.

INTERNET LINKS: www.enchantedlearning.com/subjects/dinosaurs/dinos/Plesiosaur.shtml

Reptiles of the air

The first pterosaurs, or flying reptiles, lived during the Triassic period. Their wings were made of skin that stretched from the fourth finger to the body and rear legs. Some may have had furry bodies. None of the early pterosaurs had a wingspan bigger than around 10 ft. (3m).

◀ A *Pteranodon* fossil was found with fish bones in the area of its throat. As a result, experts believe that at least part of its diet was fish. Unlike *Rhamphorhynchus*, it had a beak without teeth, like a modern bird.

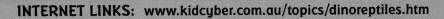

Pterodaustro strained plankton from water through its bristlelike teeth.

◀ *Pteranodon* and *Quetzalcoatlus* were two pterosaurs that lived during the Late Cretaceous. They both ate fish and flew high up in the sky, like modern-day albatross.

Dimorphodon used sharp teeth to eat insects, fish, and reptiles.

? WERE THEY DINOSAURS?

People sometimes refer to pterosaurs as dinosaurs, but although they are probably related, they are not dinosaurs.

▶ Different pterosaurs had different shaped bills, or beaks. The bill shape may have determined what they ate and how they found their food.

Dsungaripterus used the front of its bill to remove shellfish from rocks.

CREATIVE CORNER

Pteranodon kite

Use drinking straws and tape to make a diamond-shaped frame. Cut a piece of paper slightly larger than the diamond and draw a *Pteranodon* on it. Tape it to the frame. Tie a long piece of string at the bottom.

▼ *Rhamphorhynchus* was a pterosaur with a wingspan of around 6.5 ft. (2m). It lived during the Late Jurassic. It was a meat eater, and the sharp teeth in its long jaws were very useful for snatching slippery fish.

The first birds

Scientists are almost certain that modern birds evolved from dinosaurs. It is believed that the ancestors of birds were the small theropods such as *Compsognathus*. *Archaeopteryx* is the oldest bird to have been discovered so far.

Archaeopteryx

◀ *Archaeopteryx* lived during the Jurassic. Its body was like a modern crow's, but it had a long, feathered tail and big toes that pointed backward, to grip branches.

▲ Seven fossils of *Archaeopteryx* have been found in southern Germany. They show that it had teeth, finger claws, and the long, bony tail of a reptile.

Compsognathus

► *Confuciusornis* was a bird that was around the same size as *Archaeopteryx* and lived in the Early Cretaceous. It could perch like a modern bird. It ate plants and lived in large groups.

VOCABULARY

ancestor
A relative, from which an animal or person is descended.

theropod
A meat-eating dinosaur with short front legs that ran or walked on its hind legs.

125

WHY DID THEY HAVE FEATHERS?
Feathers keep birds warm and dry. Feathers were probably more important for this reason than for flying for both birds and dinosaurs.

► *Titanis* was an enormous, flesh-eating, flightless bird that became extinct at least two million years ago. It was around 8 ft. (2.5m) tall and had a huge, axlike beak. It was part of a group of birds called the "terror birds."

◄ *Caudipteryx* was a flightless animal, around the size of a turkey, that lived in the Early Cretaceous. Scientists are not sure if it was a theropod dinosaur or a bird, although most think that it was a dinosaur but possibly had ancestors that flew.

End of the dinosaurs

By the Late Cretaceous, many types of dinosaurs and other animals had died out naturally. Then, around 65 million years ago, there was a mass extinction in which all of the large land animals and many marine animals died out. Of the dinosaurs, only the theropods survived, in the form of birds.

▶ There is evidence that an asteroid hit Earth. This would have caused dust clouds and blocked out the sun's light. Earth would have been cold and dark, and plants and animals would have died.

Volcanic eruptions
Some scientists think that the extinction was caused by volcanic eruptions. Many eruptions could have caused the same effects as an asteroid strike.

WHAT IS AN ASTEROID?

An asteroid is a rocky body, like a small planet, that drifts in space. There are thousands of asteroids in the universe.

▲ Another theory is that mammals caused the end of the remaining dinosaurs by eating their eggs. It's true that the mammals were a very successful group of animals—after the dinosaurs' extinction, the next age is known as the Age of Mammals.

Survivors

The extinction killed most, but not all, animals. Marine turtles swim in our oceans today. Tuataras, which are related to both lizards and snakes, are members of a family that evolved at the time of the dinosaurs.

Green turtle

Tuatara

INTERNET LINKS: www.cotf.edu/ete/modules/msese/dinosaurflr/impact.html

Now you know!

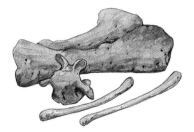

▲ *Coelophysis* was a carnivore. It probably ate other dinosaurs of its type.

◀ Pterosaurs, flying reptiles, were not dinosaurs. However, they were closely related.

▲ Fossils are bones or other remains that are preserved in rock. They tell us about animals and plants that no longer exist.

▲ Many dinosaurs had scaly skin, spines, or horns. They could have used them for attacking other animals or defending themselves from attacks.

▲ Modern birds are the descendants of some lizard-hipped dinosaurs. *Archaeopteryx* is the oldest bird found so far.

▼ Many dinosaurs ate only plants. In fact, most of the biggest dinosaurs were plant eaters.

▲ Meat eaters often had large, pointed teeth for catching and killing prey. Plant-eating dinosaurs had strong, blunt teeth for chewing.

▲ Dinosaurs died out around 65 million years ago, along with around one half of all of the animals on Earth. Scientists are still not exactly sure why.

People and Places

People have evolved, or developed, in different ways in order to cope with the landscapes that they live in and the plants and animals that are available to them. Today communication among people around the world is better than ever before, and we are gradually growing to understand and celebrate our differences.

Hockey, Canada

Snowmobiles, Iceland

North America

Europe

Eiffel Tower, Paris, France

Golden Gate Bridge, San Francisco, California

Africa

Statue of Liberty, New York City

Llamas in the Andes mountains, Peru

Our world

The world is mostly covered by water, but there are seven main areas of land, which we call continents. People live on six of these: North America, South America, Europe, Africa, Asia, and Australia.

South America

Pyramids of Giza, Egypt

Soccer, Brazil

Springbok, South Africa

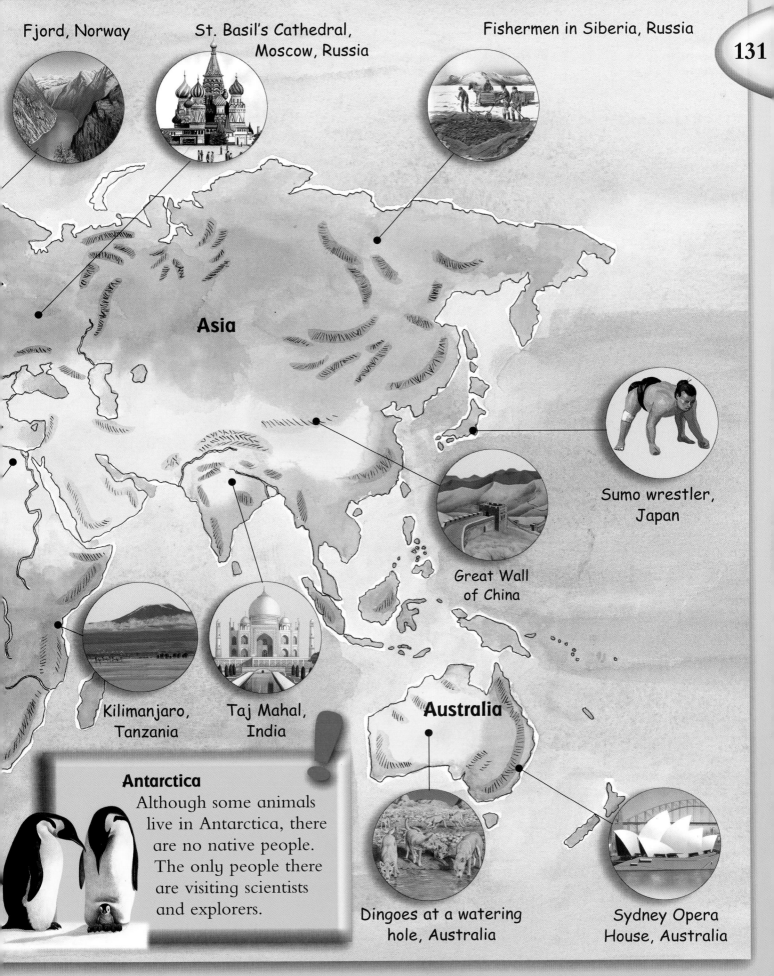

Fjord, Norway

St. Basil's Cathedral, Moscow, Russia

Fishermen in Siberia, Russia

Asia

Sumo wrestler, Japan

Great Wall of China

Kilimanjaro, Tanzania

Taj Mahal, India

Australia

Antarctica
Although some animals live in Antarctica, there are no native people. The only people there are visiting scientists and explorers.

Dingoes at a watering hole, Australia

Sydney Opera House, Australia

INTERNET LINKS: www.ipl.org/div/kidspace/browse/owd0000/

North America

The continent of North America includes Canada, the United States, and many other countries and islands. It is the third largest of the major landmasses, after Asia and Africa. The world's largest island, Greenland, is part of North America.

▼ The Grand Canyon, in Arizona, is a deep valley carved by the Colorado River over millions of years. It is 277 mi. (446km) long, and in places it is more than 5,900 ft. (1,800m) deep.

▲ The U.S. is one of the most powerful countries in the world. The Capitol building, at the top of Capitol Hill in Washington, D.C., is the U.S.'s center of government.

▲ Thanksgiving is a holiday in the U.S. when people stop to appreciate Earth and the food that it provides. It is often celebrated with a special meal.

The Kwakiutl people

This tribe, like many other tribes, lived in North America long before Europeans arrived. Many carved tall totem poles like this one to tell the story of their tribe. They celebrated by dancing and wearing masks.

▲ Canada is famous for the Royal Canadian Mounted Police, its national police force. The serving officers are often referred to as "Mounties."

◀ The Statue of Liberty, which stands in New York City harbor, was a gift from France to the U.S. It was given to celebrate the friendship between the two countries.

▲ Traveling by sleds pulled by huskies is the best way to move around in the most northern areas, where it is extremely cold.

CREATIVE CORNER

Making a cowboy doll

Cover an empty cardboard tube with brown paper. Draw, color, and cut out a head, arms, and legs and stick them onto the tube with glue. Now add clothes, a cowboy hat, and a bandanna—and maybe even a guitar!

INTERNET LINKS: www.yourchildlearns.com/us_map.htm

South America

South America is made up of 12 separate countries. This continent can be divided into three main types of landscapes. There are the Andes Mountains on the western coast, a rainforest in the northeast, and dry, grassy plains in the south.

Chocolate diet

Cocoa comes from the seeds of the cacao tree. It is used not only in chocolate bars and drinks, but also in savory dishes. It has been an important product in the economy since ancient times and may have first grown at the base of the Andes Mountains.

▶ Angel Falls in Venezuela is named after an American, James Angel. At 3,211 ft. (979m), it is the highest waterfall in the world. It drops uninterrupted for an amazing 2,647 ft. (807m).

◀ The jaguar is the largest big cat in South and Central America and is very rare in the wild. It is excellent at climbing trees and swimming and often catches fish in rivers.

◀ There are still some gauchos living on the pampas, or grasslands, of South America. Common there during the 1800s, they are great horsemen and cattle drivers.

▲ Llamas are closely related to camels. Many live high up in the Andes Mountains. They are often used for carrying goods and for their meat and fur.

▶ In Central America, Mexico's Copper Canyon system is the longest and deepest in the world. The train journey goes through valleys and forests, climbing to more than 6,800 ft. (2,100m) up the side of the canyon.

?

WHO LIVES IN COPPER CANYON?
Copper Canyon is the home of the Raramuri, or Tarahumara, people. They are skilled farmers, famous for their running abilities.

1028 1028

FNM

Europe

Europe is the second-smallest continent and contains many small countries within its borders. It has a large coastal area, and many European nations have a long history of sailing and trading. European traditions and cultures have spread to many other parts of the world.

▲ The Mediterranean region has a warm climate and beautiful beaches. Many people take vacations there.

◀ Flamenco is an exciting form of dance that began in Andalusia, Spain. This country in southern Europe shares borders with Portugal and France.

Helping with the housework?
Kobolds are types of elves, or sprites, in German folklore. They are said to do domestic chores, but may play tricks on members of the household if they are not kept happy. The metal cobalt is named after them.

◄ There are several high mountain ranges in Europe such as the Alps (shown here) and the Pyrenees. The valleys are often very fertile—suitable for growing many types of crops.

► Some of the more northern countries of Europe have snow from November till April. The people who live in these areas ski as a practical way of getting around.

◄ There are many castles in Europe. They were usually built for rich and powerful rulers. This one was built in Bavaria, Germany, for Ludwig II.

► The Netherlands is famous for its windmills, built to grind corn and drain fields of water. The country is also known for growing beautiful tulips.

Fruit ready for picking

Winemaking is an important industry in parts of Europe such as Germany, France, and Italy. Grapes ripen in the warm sun and are ready to be picked in the fall. Their juice is used to make wine and vinegar.

INTERNET LINKS: www.yourchildlearns.com/europe_map.htm

Africa

Africa is an extraordinarily varied continent. There are more than 50 countries, and they are home to many different peoples and cultures. Africa's northern coast has rich, fertile land, but south of it is the harsh Sahara Desert. Even farther south, there are areas of rainforests.

Tribal customs
In traditional African cultures, masks are often used for dancing and other rituals. This bronze mask of a ram's head is from Benin, on the western coast of the continent.

▶ There are large, bustling cities built on or near the coast. Many ships trade far and wide from these ports. Tourist ships also visit.

◀ Traditional spice markets, or souks, with their bright colors and rich scents, are still popular today in northern Africa.

▲ The island of Mauritius, off Africa's eastern coast, is known for its natural beauty, beautiful beaches, and fishing.

▼ The official color of the Masai people of Kenya and Tanzania is red. They always wear something in that color.

CAN YOU FIND?
1. a feather
2. a headdress
3. a large collar
4. bracelets
5. a necklace

▲ Many people spend a lot of their time gathering food for their families. These women are carrying millet, a type of cereal, to storehouses in their village in Burkina Faso.

▼ The nomadic tribes of Africa, who travel many miles at a time, use camels for transportation in the desert.

CREATIVE CORNER

Making an African mask
Cut a mask shape from a piece of cardboard, with holes for the eyes. Draw animal or human features on it and decorate it. You could add wool "hair" and cardboard horns. Thread a piece of string through holes to tie it around your head.

INTERNET LINKS: www.yourchildlearns.com/africa_map.htm

Asia

Asia is the largest continent, with around one third of the world's total land area. It is home to around two thirds of the world's people. In the north is a frozen area of ice. Most of the central area is desert, and in the south there are tropical beaches, islands, and rainforests.

Climbing Everest

The highest mountain, Mount Everest, is in Asia. It is 29,028 ft. (8,850m) high. The first people to climb to the top were Sir Edmund Hillary of New Zealand and Tenzing Norgay of Nepal, in 1953.

Dragon trap

In the Japanese Shinto religion, Susanowa was the god of the sea and storms. He lured an eight-headed serpent to drink eight vats of rice wine. While it drank, he cut off all of its heads and tails.

▲ People in Japan travel by train more than in any other country. The Shinkansen, or bullet train, travels at almost 190 mph (300km/h).

▶ India's famous Taj Mahal was built by Shah Jahan, a Mogul emperor of India, in memory of his wife, Mumtaz Mahal, who died in 1631.

▼ Russia plants millions of acres of wheat, barley, and other grains for food.

▲ Most of Russia's land is in Asia, but its western tip, including the capital, Moscow, is usually said to be in Europe. Moscow's famous Red Square is bordered by the Kremlin, the government's main building, and St. Basil's Cathedral.

▼ The picture below shows Chinese people working in flooded fields. Paddy fields like these are a common sight in the rice-growing countries of Southeast Asia.

WHAT IS RICE?
Rice is a member of the grass family. Its grain (part of the seed) is an important food in many parts of the world, especially in Asia.

Australia

Australia is the only country that is also a continent. Most Australians live on the eastern and southeastern coasts. The interior of the land is dry and harsh, though some aboriginal Australians, the country's original people, still live there.

▲ One of Australia's main exports is wool, which shearers cut from sheep each year.

▲ Sydney is the oldest and largest city in Australia. Its opera house is often seen as a symbol of the country.

The Great Rainbow Snake

This is an important figure in aboriginal Australian traditions. It is said that the snake created the rivers and can be seen in the sky as a rainbow.

▶ It is necessary to transport goods over very long distances in Australia. To keep costs down, companies use powerful trucks to pull several trailers at once. These are known as road trains.

▲ Some children in Australia live so far away from each other that they "go to school" using the radio or the Internet.

▲ Birds of paradise are known for their beautiful feathers. These are often used in ceremonial headdresses, like this one.

VOCABULARY

shearer

A person who cuts, or clips, the wool of a sheep or other animal.

aboriginal

Describes one of the first people to live in a particular area.

▲ On Easter Island in the Pacific Ocean, there are more than 600 giant statues, carved more than 1,000 years ago.

▲ In Rotorua, New Zealand (an island country close to Australia), geysers, or spouts, of hot water and mud shoot up from lakes.

▶ New Zealand's first inhabitants were the Maori people. They came from Polynesian islands farther north.

Languages

Being able to speak is one of the things that makes people different from other animals. Human language has taken thousands of years to develop. It allows us to share complicated ideas and to discuss subjects such as politics, philosophy, and the arts.

Semaphore

This is a language used for communicating over long distances. The sender spells out words with flags. He or she moves them to a different position for each letter or number.

▲ People and chimpanzees are very closely related. Even so, scientists have managed to teach chimps only to recognize a few simple words.

▶ Today we have many different technologies that allow us to communicate. Most of them are word based, but many of them also use sounds and images.

CAN YOU FIND?

1. a television
2. a computer
3. books
4. a telephone
5. a newspaper

中
国
人

▶ We also use our bodies to communicate our feelings. This is yet another "language" that we use. Japanese people, for example, often bow to each other as a sign of respect.

? **IS LATIN DEAD?**
Latin is a "dead" language, as nobody speaks it in day-to-day life. But it is still useful for reading old texts, which help us learn about past civilizations.

▲ Different languages are written in different ways. This set of symbols, for example, is Chinese for "Chinese people."

▶ People who have difficulty hearing or speaking often use sign language. There are signs for letters and common words.

▲ Children learn to speak and read different languages at school. They might do this by reading books or by using computers or CDs.

CREATIVE CORNER

An international collage

Using books or the Internet, find out what the word *hello* is in as many languages as you can. Make a collage of children, label each one with a language, and add a speech bubble showing the word in that language.

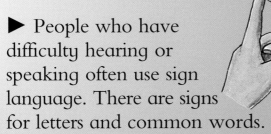

Hello

Bonjour

English

French

Ciao

Italian

Hola

Hallo

Spanish

German

INTERNET LINKS: www.planetpals.com/IKC/peacedictionary.html • www.historyforkids.org/learn/literature/

Homes

Early peoples took shelter in natural caves. Learning to build homes meant that later groups of humans could travel farther and live in places without natural shelters. The houses that we build today depend on the materials available locally as well as the types of weather against which we need to protect ourselves.

VOCABULARY
nomads
People who have no permanent homes but who travel to find food.
concrete
A building material made by mixing cement, pebbles or gravel, and water.

◀ This longhouse, on the island of Borneo in the Pacific Ocean, is on stilts to prevent it from flooding. It has storage space under the roof.

◀ The nomads of Mongolia live in yurts. These round tents are made of thick felt. They are easy to put up and take down.

Baba Yaga
In Russian myths, Baba Yaga is a wild old woman who lives in a cabin built on chicken legs, with no windows or doors. In fact, Siberian nomads build huts to store food on the stumps of trees, which look a lot like chicken legs. This is done to stop bears from getting in!

▲ In deserts and other dry areas, homes are often built out of mud. Thick walls and small windows keep them cool.

Homes can be made from all types of materials. Bricks, wood, and concrete are often used. However, igloos are made from ice, and yurts are made from felt.

▲ In hot countries, houses are often painted white to reflect the sun's heat. In Spain, people take a siesta (nap) when it is too hot to work.

▲ Brick houses like this one in Boston, Massachusetts, were originally built for one family to live in. Today many have been divided into apartments.

▲ Some people live on houseboats. These are often permanently moored, or tied up, where fresh water and electricity are available.

▲ The Inuit people of the Arctic still make bricks from ice to build their dome-shaped igloos. They do this when they go hunting.

▲ In the Alps of Europe and other snowy, mountainous regions, houses like these chalets have sloping roofs to prevent the snow from building up.

▲ This large wood-frame house is in Belize, in Central America. The timber was taken from local forests and cut into planks.

Clothes

The clothes that we wear depend on where we live, what the weather is like, and what we are planning to do. They may keep us warm or cool or protect us while we work. They can even show that we belong to a particular group of people.

▲ The Inuit people of the cold Arctic wear clothes made of tightly woven fabrics that are wind- and waterproof.

► This group of women is pounding corn to make flour for bread. Their clothes are colorful, and the baby is carried in a piece of cloth on the mother's back.

Leprechauns
There are many stories about leprechauns. These fairy shoemakers live in Ireland. It is said that if you listen very carefully, you can hear the sound of their hammers as they tap, tap, tap.

► Today we mostly dress in casual clothing. This is practical and comfortable for all types of activities. It protects us and is easy to move or run around in.

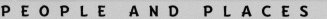

▶ At weddings in many countries, the bride is often dressed in white. In Greece, a bride traditionally has money pinned to her dress as a gift.

◀ This Indian woman is wearing a sari. This is a strip of material 16–30 ft. (5–9m) long. It is draped around the body and can be worn in various styles.

▲ Fishermen need waterproof clothing to protect them from sea spray. The bright yellow jackets shown here also make them easy to spot if they fall into the water.

CREATIVE CORNER

A doll's dress-up box
Cover an old shoebox with plain or colored paper. Now find pictures of interesting outfits, such as those of pirates, fairies, or ballerinas, in magazines. Cut them out and glue them to the box for inspiration. Glue a white label onto the lid and write your name.

Food and farming

Early peoples had to rely on what they could find or hunt for food. They often had to travel to locate enough food. But around 10,000 years ago, some people in the Middle East began to grow grains such as wheat. Farming allowed people to settle in one place and build villages and towns.

► Today huge fields of cereal crops, such as wheat, corn, and barley, are harvested using efficient machines such as combines.

◄ Today there are fewer cowboys than there used to be. However, on large ranches, lassos are still used to catch animals.

Animal farming

Like many farm animals, sheep are useful to us in more ways than one. We use the milk to drink or make cheese, the wool for clothing, and the meat for food. Sheep are easy to raise since they graze on grass in open fields.

◄ Farmers often sell their produce in markets. These Mexican women are getting ready for a busy market to open.

► Fields of sunflowers are a glorious sight. They are grown mostly for their seeds, which we eat as snacks and use in animal feed. We use oil from the seeds to cook.

◄ Cereal grains are often made into bread. There are many different types of bread. Some are light and airy, while others are flat and dense, like the pita bread shown here.

▼ Fishermen using nets can bring in millions of fish at one time. In many places, fish are raised on farms, where they are kept inside pens in the water until they are big enough to sell.

▲ Large farms often send their produce to factories, where they are sorted and packaged for sale in supermarkets or made into other products. These Albanian women are sorting apples.

INTERNET LINKS: http://tiki.oneworld.net/food/food3.html • www.kidsfarm.com/

Traditions

Cultures all over the world have special traditions, or ways of doing things, that are important to them. The traditions of a society are some of the reasons why people feel as if they belong together. They often involve music, dancing, and feasting.

The Day of the Dead

This is celebrated in Mexico and other Latin American countries. It celebrates the fact that although people die, they are also born, and the cycle of life continues.

◀ The Chinese Moon Festival is held in the fall. Families gather together to watch the full moon. They also eat special moon cakes and sing moon poems.

La Befana

In Italy, on the eve of January 6, La Befana visits all of the children to fill their socks with candy if they are good or a lump of coal if they are bad. She comes down the chimney and sweeps the floor before she leaves on her broomstick.

▲ Caribbean people celebrate many festivals. They parade through the streets in costumes, dancing and singing.

► Halloween is an ancient festival celebrating the night on which spirits are said to contact the living. Many children go trick-or-treating. They dress up in costumes and knock on neighbors' doors asking for treats, threatening to play tricks on those who do not give them anything!

▲ The carnival in Venice, Italy, has ancient origins. It is held in the spring and has a different theme every year, but masks are always worn.

► The new year in China falls in late January or early February. Chinese people all over the world celebrate it with fireworks and parades led by people in gigantic dragon costumes.

INTERNET LINKS: www.ipl.org/kidspace/browse/owd5000 • www.pitara.com/magazine/features.asp

Religions

Since ancient times, many people have believed in a god or gods. Their beliefs help them explain the world and their lives. Other religions are based around the individual rather than a god. Religions are closely tied to traditions and help people feel part of a group.

► Islam is the religion of Muslim people. Muslims believe in one god, Allah, and try to follow the rules that they believe he would like them to follow. Muslims say prayers in buildings called mosques.

▼ Christians believe in one god who sent his son, Jesus Christ, to save humankind from sin. They build churches and cathedrals in which to worship, like this one in Florence, Italy.

▲ Diwali is the Hindu festival of lights. It is held in either October or November and celebrates the triumph of good over evil and hope for humankind.

WHICH IS RIGHT?

We cannot say that any religion is the right one. Many people do not believe in a god of any type. Most people believe that we should live our lives in the way that we choose.

▲ Judaism is the religion of the Jews. It was the first religion in which members believed in only one god. Hanukkah is the celebration of lights, held in the winter.

▲ Many religions, including Hinduism, Buddhism, and Jainism, believe in a way of life rather than a god or gods. People often bring offerings to Buddhist monks (above).

The story of Buddha

A Hindu prince named Siddhartha Guatama Buddha thought that people who were truly good and pure would not have to be reborn. He decided to stop being a prince and live as good a life as he could. He had many Buddhist followers while he was alive and even more after he died.

Arts and music

People like to express themselves, and the arts provide very good ways to do this. Painting, drawing, playing or writing music, dancing, singing, and acting are all classed as arts. Today some types of arts are even used in therapy to help people overcome illnesses.

Carving wood
The Makonde people of Tanzania are famed for carving a wood called *mpingo*. They shape figures from their tribal myths as well as animals and ceremonial masks.

▼ Some of today's movies use modern technology and special effects. However, movies are usually made with actors and traditional film sets.

Mermaids
These mythical sea creatures have the heads and upper bodies of women and the tails of fish. They are sometimes said to sing so sweetly that sailors become entranced, fall into the ocean, and drown.

▲ India has a strong dance tradition. Indian dance is enjoyed all over the world because of its use in popular "Bollywood" movies.

Shadow puppet theater

Javanese folktales are acted out in shadows on a screen. Highly skilled puppeteers move puppets, which can be more than 3 ft. (1m) tall, using long rods. A light behind the puppets casts shadows onto a screen.

▲ A gamelan is a set of Indonesian instruments. It often includes xylophones, drums, and gongs, and sometimes there are flutes and strings. The instruments are built and tuned to play together.

◀ Valuable works of art and old objects are often kept in museums and art galleries. The staff looks after the items to preserve them. Everyone can visit to see and learn more about them.

► An orchestra is a group of different types of instruments and the people who play them. It is directed by a conductor.

▲ Ballet is a formal style of dance that began in Europe more than 300 years ago. It uses special gestures, developed from mime, to tell a story.

INTERNET LINKS: www.artsology.com/home.php • www.kidsolr.com/arts_music/index.html

Sports

Sports are games that involve physical skills of some type. People take part in sports for many reasons—to stay in shape, to compete against others, or just for fun. Many modern sports, such as running, wrestling, and archery, have developed from skills that people originally needed to survive in the world.

Olympic Games
The modern Olympics are based on games held in ancient Greece more than 2,000 years ago. They take place every two years.

◀ Cycling is a popular sport for all ages, mostly because it does not need a special stadium, a track, or equipment besides the bicycle itself and a safety helmet.

▶ The world record for speed skiing is more than 155 mph (250km/h). It is the second-fastest nonmotorized sport after skydiving.

▲ In track events, runners compete over different distances. Only in the shortest races do the runners sprint, or run as fast as possible, for the whole race.

▶ Grand Prix racecars are designed for speed. They are very light, with powerful engines, and are so low that the drivers have to lie almost flat in their seats.

▲ In cricket, the batting team tries to score "runs." The fielding team tries to stop them or get them out.

▲ In basketball, two teams of five players each compete to score points by throwing a ball through a hoop.

▲ Martial arts, such as karate and judo, began in Eastern countries. Boxing and wrestling began in the West.

▲ In soccer, each team tries to score goals by kicking a ball into a net.

CREATIVE CORNER

Making a bowling alley outside

Fill some empty plastic bottles halfway with water or sand and replace the caps. Stand them upright a few inches in front of a wall. Play with a friend and see how many "pins" you can knock over at one time by rolling a ball at them.

INTERNET LINKS: http://www.super-kids.com/sports.html • www.museum.upenn.edu/new/olympics/olympicintro.html

Now you know!

▲ Many celebrations involve music and dance. They often have festive clothes and masks, too.

▲ Cocoa, which we use for chocolate, has been an important crop in South America since ancient times.

▲ Venezuela's Angel Falls is the highest waterfall at almost 3,300 ft. (1,000m) high.

▼ Nomads are people who move from place to place in search of food.

▲ The Mounties are a special police force in Canada. They use horses to travel around.

► The Great Rainbow Snake is an ancient god said by the aborigines of Australia to have created rivers.

▲ People have learned to cope with extreme temperatures such as the cold in the Arctic and far northern regions of Earth.

◄ People all over the world celebrate some of the same things— for example, the holiday of Halloween on October 31.

People Through Time

Through history, we find out how people lived long ago, discovering and exploring the world around them. History tells us how they ate, dressed, made music and art, and told stories. This helps us understand why we live the way we do today.

Prehistory

Apelike creatures developed in Africa millions of years ago. Several species learned how to walk on two legs and even use tools. Around 400,000 years ago, some of these creatures developed into early forms of human beings. Around 130,000 years ago, modern types of humans appeared. They then spread to other parts of the world.

Stone Age

The first people chipped hard stones, such as flint, until they were sharp. That is why this period is called the Stone Age. They also used wood, bone, and horn.

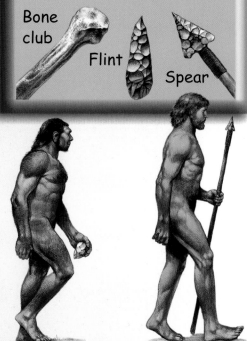

Bone club

Flint

Spear

Australopithecus (southern ape) 5 to 1 million years ago

Homo habilis (handy human) 2.2 to 1.6 million years ago

Homo erectus (upright human) 2 to 0.4 million years ago

Homo neanderthalensis (early wise human) 200,000 to 30,000 years ago

Homo sapiens (modern wise human) 130,000 years ago to the present

▲ Early creatures in the human family could run and climb. They were intelligent, with big brains. They were good at gripping objects. They made simple tools and weapons and used them to hunt and gather food.

Is anybody out there?

Did prehistoric ape-men survive into modern times? There are many tales of strange beasts living in remote forests or mountains. A legend from the Himalayas tells of a creature called the yeti, or "abominable snowman."

▼ Inside these caves in France, people made paintings of wild animals more than 15,000 years ago. Many early peoples made their homes in caves.

▲ In prehistoric times there were long ice ages around the world. People survived by hunting animals such as the woolly mammoth.

CAN YOU FIND?
1. a lamp burning animal fat
2. clothes made from animal skins
3. colors being mixed
4. wooden poles

First civilizations

People learned how to tame animals and grow crops in western Asia more than 12,000 years ago. Villages grew into busy towns and cities. Some cities conquered others, creating countries and empires. People learned to write and understand mathematics and to trade, govern, and pass laws. These were the world's first civilizations.

Clever inventions
Inventions that changed the world were made in ancient Iraq more than 5,000 years ago. The first writing was made up of marks pressed into soft clay. The first carts used heavy wheels made of wood.

Writing on clay

Wooden wheel

◀ Powerful cities developed in Sumer, a region of what is now Iraq. The people grew powerful by trading along the rivers. They built many large cities and used slaves to do work.

Gilgamesh the superhero
The people of Sumer liked to tell stories about Gilgamesh, the powerful and proud king of the city of Uruk. Among other adventures, he attacked the monster Humbaba and killed the Bull of Heaven that had been sent to destroy him. But he never found out the secret of how to live forever.

▲ This is the oldest known board game in the world. It was made before 2600 B.C. and placed in a royal tomb in Ur, one of the greatest cities of Sumer.

◀ Copper and tin were mined and traded in western Asia. By 3500 B.C. these metals were being heated and mixed to make bronze.

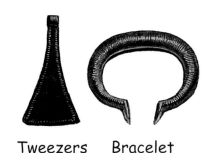

Pin   Tweezers   Bracelet

◀ Iron is a tougher and harder metal than bronze. It was used in what is now Turkey by around 1300 B.C. People called the Hittites conquered large areas of west Asia at this time using iron weapons.

▶ The Assyrians were a western Asian people who conquered many lands from the 1100s to the 600s B.C. Their fierce armies attacked city walls with archers, ladders, towers, and battering rams. The Assyrian kings built fine palaces with libraries and gardens.

INTERNET LINKS: www.kidsnewsroom.org/elmer/infoCentral/frameset/civilizations/meso/index.html

The Egyptians

The Nile River flows through the deserts of Egypt in North Africa. The river flooded each year, leaving a rich mud. Farmers grew crops on the riverbanks, providing food for people in the towns and cities. Egypt was a powerful kingdom, with fine tombs and palaces.

Nut of the stars
The Egyptian sky goddess was named Nut. Egyptian wall paintings show her arching over the earth god, Geb. Her body is covered with stars. Egyptians believed that each morning Nut gave birth to the sun god, Ra, and swallowed him again each evening.

◀ More than 4,500 years ago the Egyptians buried their kings, the pharaohs, in huge pyramids. These pointed stone monuments were built by thousands of laborers, who toiled in the hot desert sun.

CAN YOU FIND?
1. an injured worker
2. a ramp
3. a wooden sled
4. a wooden box
5. a dog

▲ In front of the pyramids in Giza is a sphinx, a statue of a lion with a human head. The head may show the face of the pharaoh Khafra.

▼ The Egyptians used reed boats to hunt hippopotamuses in the Nile River. The animals were a nuisance because they trampled crops along the riverbanks.

▲ Tutankhamen was a young pharaoh who died in 1325 B.C. His body was preserved to make a mummy. It was wrapped and covered with a gold mask. Then it was put inside human-shaped coffins in a stone box.

◄ The Egyptians worshiped hundreds of gods. Ra was the sun god, and Osiris was the god of death and rebirth. Isis, his wife, was the mother goddess, while Anubis was the god of the dead.

Ra   Osiris   Isis   Anubis

The ancient East

Great civilizations developed around the Indus River, in what is now Pakistan, as well as in India, China, and Southeast Asia. For thousands of years, this area produced great inventions, works of art, books, statues, temples and palaces, and scientific discoveries. There was also long-distance trade in spices, silk, jade, and ivory.

▲ From around 3300 to 1600 B.C., Harappa was one of the great cities of the Indus valley. It had houses made of bricks, drains, toilets, bathtubs, and wide streets. Around 40,000 people lived there.

▼ The first emperor of all of China, Qin Shi Huangdi, died in 210 B.C. Placed around his tomb were thousands of life-size model soldiers. He thought that they would guard his body against evil spirits. The ghostly army was discovered in 1974.

Mother of Dragons
The Chinese tell of a woman who found a magic egg beside a river. Five dragons hatched, and she became known as Long Mu, Mother of Dragons. After she died, the dragons turned into wise men called the Five Scholars.

▼ For more than 1,000 years, walls were built along the northern borders of China to defend the empire against invaders. Together they made up the Great Wall of China.

Trading seal

Merchants from the city of Mohenjo-Daro in the Indus valley used seals like this one to mark their goods around 4,000 years ago. They traded with the cities of western Asia.

▼ China grew into the most powerful empire on Earth. Its cities had canals, bridges, roads, and high towers called pagodas. Its markets sold rice, wheat, and tea.

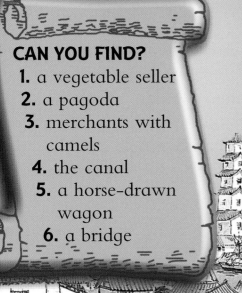

CAN YOU FIND?

1. a vegetable seller
2. a pagoda
3. merchants with camels
4. the canal
5. a horse-drawn wagon
6. a bridge

The Greeks

Between around 2000 and 146 B.C. great civilizations developed in Greece. The Greeks also settled around the Mediterranean Sea and the Black Sea. They were great thinkers, politicians, writers, athletes, sculptors, sailors, and warriors. In the 300s B.C., Greeks ruled most of western Asia and also Egypt.

Time's up!
Athens allowed its citizens to govern themselves. This was called democracy. There were assemblies, councils, and public law courts. Speakers in court had a time limit. They could speak until the water ran out of a pot that had a hole in it.

◀ Athens was one of the greatest Greek cities. In the center of Athens was a rocky hill called the Acropolis. A splendid temple called the Parthenon, in which there was a giant statue of Athena, the Greek goddess of wisdom, stood there.

▶ The Greeks had many gods. Hermes was their messenger; Aphrodite, the goddess of love; Zeus, the king of the gods; and Hera, the queen. Demeter was the goddess of the earth, and Hades was god of the underworld.

Hermes   Aphrodite   Zeus   Hera   Demeter   Hades

◄ A fleet of Greek ships prepares for war. These ships were called triremes and had three banks of oars as well as sails. The pointed fronts of the ships were used to ram enemy boats and sink them.

► The Greeks built open-air theaters in many cities. The actors wore masks. All of the parts were played by men. Sad plays were called tragedies. Funny plays were called comedies.

▲ One Greek city-state was called Sparta. Spartan children were raised to be tough. The boys were trained to be soldiers.

CREATIVE CORNER

Making a Greek shield
Draw a circle on a piece of cardboard. Cut it out. Now draw a leaping dolphin and paint it blue and the background yellow. Use a black marker to draw a border. Cut a wide strip of cardboard and glue it to the back as the handle.

INTERNET LINKS: www.bbc.co.uk/schools/ancientgreece/main_menu.shtml

The Romans

The Italian city of Rome was first settled around 753 B.C. Within 500 years, the Romans had conquered most of Italy. They went on to rule a huge empire that stretched across Europe, western Asia, and North Africa. They built long, straight roads from one city to another. The Roman Empire lasted until A.D. 476.

▲ Roman dress included cloaks, tunics, shawls, long dresses, leather boots, and sandals. Most clothes were made from wool.

◀ Most of Europe was the home of Celtic peoples such as the Gauls and the Britons. The Romans fought against the Celts and conquered many of their lands.

Saturn's holiday

The Romans believed that the god Saturn was driven from the heavens by Jupiter and hid himself in Rome. Every winter, a holiday called Saturnalia was held in Rome in his honor. It was marked by feasting, merrymaking, practical jokes, and presents. Slaves and masters switched places for the day.

▲ The Romans loved the public baths. There they could plunge into cold tubs and hot pools and have massages. They could exercise or just talk to their friends.

Making a tortoise

The Roman army was divided into groups called legions. When soldiers of a legion were attacking a fort, they sometimes formed a tight band and placed shields around and over their bodies. This was called making a "tortoise."

▲ Important men wore long robes called togas. These two men are doing business in Rome's forum, the city center.

▼ The Coliseum was a big stadium in the middle of Rome. It could hold around 50,000 spectators. Instead of sports, they watched horrible shows in which wild animals and people were cruelly killed.

◄ Gladiators were trained fighters who fought to the death in the arena. The emperor would decide if their lives would be spared.

The Vikings

Scandinavia is a name given to the countries of Sweden, Denmark, and Norway. The people who farmed and fished there around 1,200 years ago were called Vikings. They were great explorers, reaching North America and trading from Russia to Iraq.

Rune stones

The Vikings built stone memorials carved with their own type of writing and decorated with swirling patterns. They used a 16-letter alphabet, with letters called runes.

Sleipnir the swift

The Vikings loved to tell stories about gods, giants, and magical beasts. Sleipnir was the horse ridden by Odin, the father of the gods. Sleipnir had eight legs and could ride like the wind, over land or through the air. He was said to have been born from Svadilfari, the horse of the giants, and Loki, the mischief-maker.

◄ The Vikings were fierce warriors, feared all across Europe. They carried swords, axes, spears, and round shields. When two Vikings quarreled, they might have been ordered to settle the argument with a fight to the death.

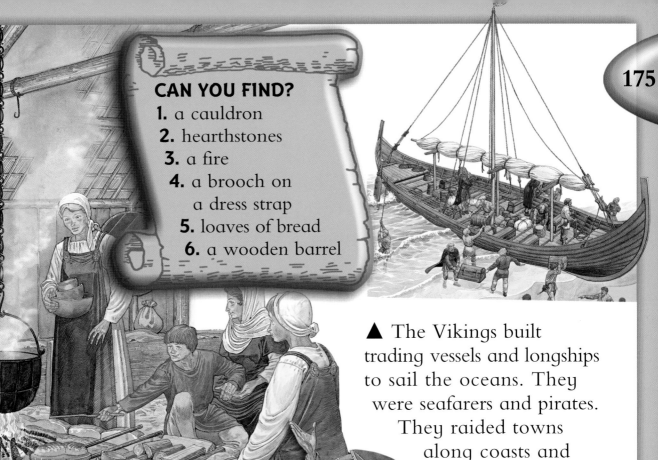

CAN YOU FIND?
1. a cauldron
2. hearthstones
3. a fire
4. a brooch on a dress strap
5. loaves of bread
6. a wooden barrel

▲ The Vikings built trading vessels and longships to sail the oceans. They were seafarers and pirates. They raided towns along coasts and rivers, taking gold, cattle, and slaves.

▲ The Vikings lived in farming settlements and built long, low houses. There was a fire for cooking inside. Smoke escaped through a hole in the roof. Families gathered around the fire after a hard day's work.

▶ Viking warriors loved to feast and drink. Poets would sing the praises of the chief at feasts in the hope of a reward. They would also tell stories and riddles.

The Middle Ages

In Europe, the thousand years between the end of the Roman Empire and the beginning of the modern age are known as the Middle Ages. This was a time when kings and queens built castles and big churches called cathedrals. Most people followed the Christian religion, although the Moors of southern Spain were Muslims, and Jews lived in many towns.

VOCABULARY

cathedral
The most important church in a region, run by a bishop.

plague
A terrible disease that spreads from one person to another.

◀ Poor peasants had to work hard in the fields. They had to provide food for the lord in the local manor house or the castle. In times of war, they had to fight for him. In return, he promised to protect them from attacks.

Lord

Monk

DID CHILDREN GO TO SCHOOL?
Many children worked on the land or learned a trade. Most could not read or write. A few were taught by monks at church schools.

Peasants

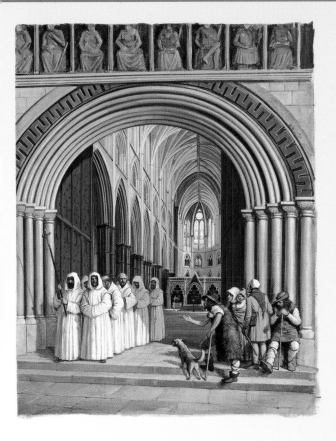

▲ The Black Death was a terrible plague that swept across Asia and Europe in the 1340s. It was spread by rat fleas. Thousands of people died.

▲ Churches were built in every town and city. The head of the church was the pope, who lived in Rome, Italy. People called pilgrims traveled long distances to pray at holy places such as Rome or Santiago de Compostela, in Spain.

▶ Many long and terrible wars were fought during the Middle Ages. Here, a Spanish army led by a famous knight named El Cid is capturing the city of Valencia from the Moors. The year is 1094.

INTERNET LINKS: www.historyforkids.org/learn/medieval/ • www.learner.org/exhibits/middleages/

Knights and castles

During the Middle Ages, wars were fought by horsemen in armor. They were called knights, and they carried shields, swords, and long spears called lances. Kings and lords lived in castles, which were hard to attack. Many castles were built with thick walls of stone.

VOCABULARY

tournament
A mock battle fought between knights with blunt (dull) weapons.

siege
The act of surrounding a castle and cutting off its supplies, forcing it to surrender.

◀ At festivals called tournaments, knights would show off their fighting skills in mock battles. Each would try to knock the other off his horse. The knights would wear fancy armor and helmets.

King Arthur and the Knights of the Round Table

Arthur was probably a warrior who lived in Great Britain in the 500s. After he died, amazing stories were told about him. By the 1100s, Arthur was being described as a great king whose knights sat at a round table. They were said to be adventurous, brave, and honorable. Many real-life knights wanted to be like the ones in King Arthur's court.

CAN YOU FIND?

1. a well
2. a musician
3. a bed
4. a spiral staircase
5. a monk
6. a knight on horseback

▶ During a siege, one army would surround and try to capture a castle, using ladders and giant catapults. The other army would shoot arrows and throw rocks.

◀ A castle was a home as well as a place for fighting. This is an early castle that is a simple, strong tower. Later castles had round walls with many layers of defense.

CREATIVE CORNER

Your coat of arms

Copy a shield shape onto a piece of paper and divide it into four parts. Draw a ribbon underneath and an emblem in each quarter. Then color the emblems and the background. Now write your motto (saying) in the ribbon.

INTERNET LINKS: www.castles.org/Kids_Section/Castle_Story/ • www.knightsandarmor.com/

Explorers

During the Middle Ages, Arab and Chinese seafarers explored the Indian Ocean and the coast of east Africa. Polynesians explored the islands of the Pacific Ocean. Europeans sailed around Africa to India. By the 1500s, Europeans were sailing around the world.

North, south, east, west
Explorers use compasses to find their way. The magnetic iron needle always points north. Compasses were invented in China and were being used by sailors in the 1100s.

▲ Marco Polo (1254–1324) and his family were merchants from Venice, Italy. They traveled all the way to China. They were presented to the emperor and saw many amazing sights.

▶ Ibn Battuta was born in Morocco in 1304. He spent almost 30 years of his life exploring Egypt, Arabia, India, Southeast Asia, China, and west Africa. He wrote about his adventures.

Dreaming of El Dorado
In the 1500s, Spanish soldiers were exploring South America. They heard rumors of a ruler called El Dorado, "the Golden One," whose body was covered in gold dust. His kingdom was said to be full of fabulous riches . . . but no such land really existed.

► Ferdinand Magellan left Spain in 1519. He traveled through icy waters off South America before reaching the Pacific Ocean. His crew sailed around the world, but he was killed along the way.

▲ This Spanish ship was called *Santa Maria*. Its captain was an Italian named Christopher Columbus. In 1492, he sailed across the Atlantic Ocean to discover the New World—the Americas.

◄ For hundreds of years, pirates attacked ships in the Caribbean Sea and other parts of the world. They stole any treasures that they could find onboard. They were often very cruel and violent people.

CREATIVE CORNER

Making a treasure-island map

Draw the outline of your imaginary island. Mark beaches, bays, palm trees, hills, and a river. Give them all names. Draw compass points. Decorate the map with pictures of old sailing ships or sea monsters.

INTERNET LINKS: www.metmuseum.org/explore/Marco/index.html • www.all-kids.us/ships-page.html

The Inca

Many important civilizations developed in South America. In the 1400s, the empire of the Inca ruled most of the Pacific coast and the Andes Mountains. It was conquered by Spanish soldiers in the 1530s.

▼ The Inca emperor made offerings to Inti, the sun god. People believed that the emperor was descended from the sun and the empress from the moon.

String science

The Inca used a band of knotted strings in different colors to keep records and do math. It was called a quipu. Learning to use a quipu was very complicated.

WHY WERE METALS HOLY?

The Inca called gold the "sweat of the sun" and silver the "tears of the moon." They were the metals of the gods.

▶ Tunics and shawls were woven from the hair of animals. Llama hair was quite coarse, but alpaca hair was soft and silky.

▲ The Inca emperor Atahualpa was captured by Spanish soldiers in November 1532. His people gave the soldiers a fortune in gold, but the Spanish still murdered him the following summer.

▲ The Inca town of Machu Picchu was built high up in the mountains. It had houses for farmers, craftworkers and soldiers, a square, a temple, and a palace. Fields were cut from the mountainside.

CREATIVE CORNER

Making a mask
Draw an outline of a mask to match the size of your face. Cut out eyeholes. Draw the eyebrows, nose, mouth, and ears. Make holes for the string.

INTERNET LINKS: www.nationalgeographic.com/ngkids/games/brainteaser/inca/inca.html

The Aztecs

The lands of Mexico and Central America also saw many civilizations develop. The most powerful empire in the 1400s was ruled by the Aztecs. Their capital city, Tenochtitlán, was built on an island in a lake. More than 250,000 people lived there. It was destroyed by Spanish soldiers in 1521.

Worship
The Aztecs worshiped many gods. There were gods of war, of rain, of the springtime, and of death. There were goddesses of lakes, of corn, and of the hearth.

◀ The Aztecs built platforms of mud, sticks, and reeds in the lake and turned them into farmland. They grew corn, sweet potatoes, beans, tomatoes, and chili peppers.

The eagle and the cactus
The Aztec people originally lived far to the north. They were told by the war god to travel south. The god told them to make their home wherever they saw an eagle land on a cactus plant. At last they saw their eagle— on a swampy island in Lake Texcoco.

▶ Aztec nobles lived in beautiful houses and palaces. These had courtyards, bedrooms, and kitchens. Aztecs liked to entertain important guests with splendid feasts.

◀ The weapons of an Aztec warrior were edged with a sharp black stone called obsidian. There were two top fighting groups called the Eagles and the Jaguars. This is an Eagle warrior.

▼ A huge pyramid towered over the center of Tenochtitlán. Steps led up to temples on the top, where thousands of prisoners of war were sacrificed to the gods on stone altars.

▲ The Aztecs liked to play a ball game called *tlachtli*. The rubber ball could not be handled or kicked. It had to be bounced off the body. The goal was to get it through a high stone ring.

Age of empires

Between the 1500s and the 1900s, the Europeans created huge empires in Africa, Asia, and Australia as well as the Americas. Sometimes they settled in the lands that they ruled. Sometimes they mined metals or planted crops to make themselves rich. The people they ruled often stayed poor.

▲ The Turkish Ottoman Empire lasted from 1299 to 1922. It ruled the Middle East, North Africa, and southeast Europe. One of its greatest rulers was Suleiman the Magnificent. Here, he is attacking the city of Vienna, Austria.

▼ Napoleon was a French emperor who conquered most of Europe in the 1800s. He was defeated in 1815, but France still went on to gain a huge empire in Africa and Asia.

CAN YOU FIND?
1. a rifle
2. a bayonet
3. a French flag
4. a soldier's pack
5. a sword
6. a tricorn hat

► Great Britain founded colonies in North America. During the American Revolution, the colonists broke away from British rule. The rebels captured Fort Ticonderoga in New York in 1757.

◄ In South America, the colonists also fought against European rule. Rebels waged a big battle against the Spanish in Ayacucho, Peru, in 1824 and defeated them. Famous freedom fighters included Simón Bolívar.

▼ Big, fast sailing ships called clippers carried tea from China and wool from Australia back to Great Britain from the 1870s to 1890s. Soon the clippers were replaced by steamships.

Queen Victoria

This queen ruled over Great Britain from 1837 to 1901. She also became the empress of India. She ruled over the British Empire, the largest that the world had ever known. At its height, the British Empire covered one fourth of all of the land on Earth.

INTERNET LINKS: http://encyclopedia.kids.net.au/page/br/British_Empire

Age of industry

In the 1700s and 1800s, new machines were invented, many powered by steam. Coal was mined, and engineers figured out new ways of making iron and steel. This was the age of industry, when smoky cities and big factories developed near the new canals and railroads.

VOCABULARY

industry
The world of work; the making and selling of goods.

factory
A building where products are made or processed on a large scale.

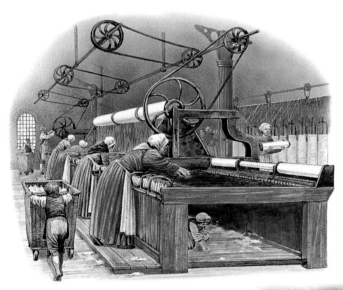

▶ The Eiffel Tower was built out of iron in 1887. It rose high up above the city of Paris, France. People learned new ways of building. The first skyscrapers were being built in North America.

▲ Cloth was no longer woven at home, but in mills that could produce large amounts very quickly. Men, women, and children worked long hours for very little pay.

◀ Locomotives were first used to pull steam trains in 1804. Railroads were soon crossing the world. This "iron horse" puffed its way across North America.

▲ This cast-iron bridge was the first of its kind. It was built across the Severn River in Ironbridge, England, and opened in 1781. The age of industry began in Great Britain but soon spread across northern Europe and North America.

▲ This huge steam hammer was invented in 1842. It could beat and shape red-hot iron.

▼ In Europe many people were poor and hungry during the 1800s. Some left their homes to make a new start in distant lands. These people have crossed the ocean to the United States. Their ship is passing the Statue of Liberty in New York City.

Modern world

The past 100 years have seen the age of the automobile, the airplane, and space rockets. They have seen the birth of radio, movies, television, and computers. New medicines have saved millions of lives. However, this has also been an age of terrible wars.

▲ An armor-plated tank crosses a muddy battlefield in France during World War I. Millions of young men from many parts of the world died between 1914 and 1918.

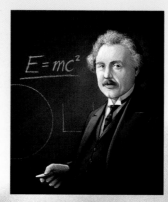

Albert Einstein

▲ In the 1900s, scientists, such as Albert Einstein, made discoveries about how our universe works. This knowledge was used to design fearsome new weapons. Nuclear bombs were dropped (above, left) at the end of World War II (1939–1945).

▼ People dreamed of flying for hundreds of years. At last, in 1903 in the United States, that dream came true. Today's big jets can take passengers huge distances in only a few hours.

▶ This weather satellite circles our planet, keeping an eye on storms below. The first space satellite was launched in 1957. By 1969, humans were standing on the Moon. The next great space challenge is to send people to Mars.

◀ Many of the things in this bedroom would have been unknown to a girl from the 1800s. They include the computer, the radio, and the electric light, as well as plastic and nylon.

▶ Cars and trucks have made our lives much easier, but like other types of transportation, they fill the air with harmful gases. These gases are damaging our planet.

CREATIVE CORNER

Making a time capsule
Choose items such as photographs that will tell people in the future how we live today. Place them inside a sealed container. Put your name, age, and address inside the time capsule. Bury it underground.

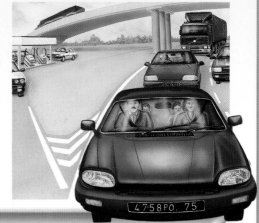

Now you know!

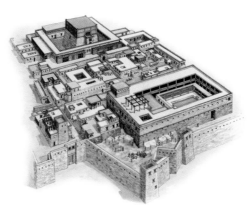

▲ In prehistoric times, people lived by hunting. They used tools and weapons made of stone.

▲ The ancient Chinese built canals, walls, and great cities. They created many useful inventions.

▲ Castles and cathedrals were built in Europe during the Middle Ages. At this time, the Inca and the Aztecs were building cities in the Americas.

▲ By 5,500 years ago, people in western Asia were building towns, writing, and using wheels to travel.

▲ The ancient Egyptians lived in North Africa. They built huge pyramids more than 4,500 years ago.

▲ More than 2,000 years ago, the Greeks and Romans produced many thinkers, sculptors, poets, mathematicians, soldiers, engineers, and athletes.

▲ From the 1500s to the 1800s, powerful empires ruled large areas of the world.

▼ In the 1700s and 1800s, many new cities, factories, and railroads were built. Amazing new technology was developed in the 1900s.

My Body

Have you ever wondered how your body works? Your body is a complicated machine, with all of the parts working together. Your body never stops working, even when you are fast asleep at night. Your heart and brain keep going 24 hours a day for your entire life.

The human body

Your body is an incredible machine. It has thousands of parts that work together to keep you alive. Each group of parts, also called a system, has a particular job. For example, your muscles keep your body moving, and your blood carries oxygen and nutrients throughout your body. All of the different systems must work correctly so that you can stay healthy.

◀ The color of our hair, skin, and eyes may be different, but whatever we look like, our bodies work in exactly the same way. We are all human beings.

▲ Your bones make up a structure called a skeleton. This protects your soft internal organ

VOCABULARY

organ
A part of your body that does a particular job.

nerve cell
A tiny living unit that carries messages to and from your brain.

▲ Muscles are attached to your bones. They pull on the bones, and this makes you move.

▲ Your brain contains billions of nerve cells, called neurons, that send messages around your body.

▲ Arteries carry blood away from your heart, and veins carry blood back to your heart.

◄ The human body can survive in extreme conditions. Mountain climbers protect themselves from the freezing cold by wearing protective clothing.

Pinocchio

In the story of Pinocchio, a toy maker named Geppetto wishes for his wooden puppet to become a real boy. His wish comes true, and Pinocchio comes to life. He has many amazing adventures.

Skin

Your skin covers your whole body, protecting it and keeping it at the right temperature. Skin is actually your body's biggest organ. It is alive on the inside, but dead on the outside. The dead layer keeps your body waterproof and stops it from being attacked and invaded by harmful bacteria.

▼ The outer layer of your skin is called the epidermis. It is covered with hairs and pores, which are tiny holes to let out your sweat. Underneath the epidermis is a living layer of skin called the dermis.

HOW MUCH SKIN DO I HAVE?
Your skin grows along with you. When you are an adult, you will have around 22 sq. ft. (2m²) of skin.

Hair   Sweat pore

Epidermis
Dermis
Sweat gland

Skin color
Everyone's skin contains a coloring substance called melanin. This tans the skin a darker color. Dark skin contains more melanin than fair skin.

X
The hot sun can burn your skin!

▲ As skin ages, it gets wrinkled and less elastic. Pinch yourself to see how quickly your skin falls back into place. Old skin takes much longer.

▲ Freckles are made where there are concentrated amounts of melanin in the skin. They increase and get darker in sunny weather and then fade during the winter.

▼ When you are cold, the muscles at the base of your hairs contract, making your hairs stand up on end. Small bumps, called goose bumps, appear all over your skin.

▲ Your skin is the part of your body that is exposed to the outside world. It is easy to scratch, cut, or bruise it. However, your skin heals very quickly when it is damaged.

CREATIVE CORNER

Taking fingerprints

Use an ink pad to make your fingertip inky. Then look at the finger through a magnifying glass. The swirling pattern of lines on your fingerprint is unique. This means that no one else in the world has exactly the same fingerprint as you do.

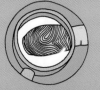

INTERNET LINKS: www.kidshealth.org/kid/body/skin_SW.html

Hair

198

Hair grows all over your body, except on the soles of your feet, the palms of your hands, and your lips. Your hair grows from tiny pockets in your skin called follicles. The shape of these follicles affects how curly your hair is. Hair dies as it grows out from your skin, so it does not hurt when it is cut.

◄ Straight hair grows out from follicles with round openings. In a cross section, straight hair is round shaped.

◄ Wavy hair is oval when seen in a cross section. This is because it grows out of oval hair follicles.

◄ Curly hair is flat in shape, because it grows out from follicles that are shaped like slots.

Rapunzel
In the fairy tale of Rapunzel, an evil witch traps a beautiful princess at the top of a tall tower. Rapunzel lets down her long, blond hair so that a brave prince can climb up the tower to rescue her.

HOW MANY HAIR FOLLICLES DO I HAVE?
You have hair follicles all over your body. As you get older, you get more hairy! Adults have around 20 million hair follicles.

Nails

Your nails never stop growing and need to be cut, just like your hair. Boys' fingernails usually grow faster than girls' fingernails, and everyone's nails grow more during the summer. As you get older, your nails do not grow as fast.

Hard as nails

The horns of a ram are like your hair and nails! Human hair and nails contain keratin. This tough protein is also found in animal horns, claws, and hooves, as well as in the shafts of birds' feathers.

VOCABULARY

cuticle
The protective layer of skin at the base of your fingernail.

circulation
The movement of blood around your body as your heart pumps.

◀ Your fingernails grow around half a millimeter every week and take six months to grow from base to tip. Fingernails grow faster than toenails.

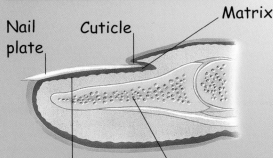

Nail plate   Cuticle   Matrix

Nail bed   Finger bone

▲ Fingernails grow out from the matrix, which is underneath the cuticle. As new cells grow, older cells are pushed up and out in the form of a hard nail.

Healthy nails

Some people like to paint their nails, but this may cover up important clues about their health. For example, hard or brittle nails may mean that a person has poor circulation, an infection, or a problem with his or her diet.

199

Teeth

Children have 20 milk teeth, and grownups have 32 adult teeth. The part of a tooth that you can see is called the crown. It is covered with a hard, white material called enamel. The part of a tooth that is hidden underneath the gum is the root. The soft inner part of a tooth contains blood vessels and nerves and is called the pulp. People should take care of their teeth—they have to last a very long time.

▲ Milk contains a substance called calcium, which helps teeth grow. Drinking a lot of milk and water and eating healthy food strengthens teeth.

The tooth fairy
In many countries, there is a popular tradition. If a milk tooth falls out, the child puts it under his or her pillow. The tooth fairy will take it away to her castle and leave them money in return.

Milk teeth

Gum

Adult teeth

Jawbone

▲ Your first teeth are called your milk teeth. These teeth start to fall out around the age of six. They are gradually pushed out by the adult teeth that move up or down from the gums.

Brushing your teeth

Small pieces of leftover food in the mouth mix with saliva to form plaque. This sticks and can cause tooth decay. Brushing your teeth after every meal can stop this from happening.

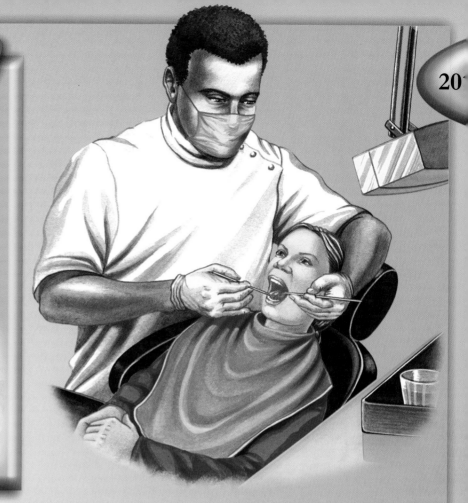

▲ Regular visits to the dentist for checkups are vital. Dentists can spot if there is something wrong with your teeth or gums. They can give the right treatment or advice before the problem gets worse.

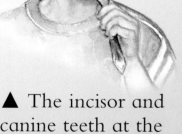

▲ The incisor and canine teeth at the front of the mouth bite into food. The strong, flat molars at the back are used for chewing. Food is easier to digest if it is fully chewed.

CREATIVE CORNER

Tooth experiment

When a milk tooth falls out, put it into a glass. Then pour in some soda. See what happens to the tooth after a day and again after a week. You will see why soda is so bad for your teeth.

INTERNET LINKS: www.adha.org/kidstuff/index.html

Bones

All of your bones link to form your skeleton, which supports your body and protects its organs. Some of the bones are very big, while others are tiny. You were born with around 300 bones, but as you grow up, some of the bones fuse together. Adults have around 200 bones.

VOCABULARY

x-ray
A special photograph of the inside of the body.

cartilage
Tissue found in joints and in the soft parts of the skeleton.

▲ The point where two bones meet is called a joint. A layer of tissue called cartilage covers the bones in a joint so that they move together smoothly. The biggest joint in your body is your knee.

◄ Bones are strong, but they can break. Doctors take x-rays to look at broken bones. Children's bones are still growing, so they heal more quickly than adults' bones.

CREATIVE CORNER

A dancing skeleton
Draw a skeleton on some cardboard, leaving a gap between the main joints. Cut out the bones and then use brass fasteners to attach them together again. Make your skeleton move its arms and legs.

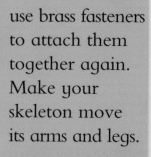

Muscles

Muscles are attached to your bones, and they make your body move. They pull but they cannot push, so most of the muscles have to work in pairs or groups. When you take a step, you use around 200 different muscles! When you are sitting still, muscles are making organs work inside your body.

▶ Your tongue is made up of a group of very strong and flexible muscles. You can move your tongue to speak, eat, and make silly faces!

◀ The muscles that you can move are called voluntary muscles. There are around 660 of them in the human body. They heat up when they move, which keeps you warm.

Biceps relaxing

Biceps pulling

Triceps relaxing

Triceps pulling

▲ When you bend your arm, your biceps muscle pulls and your triceps muscle relaxes. When you straighten your arm, the triceps pulls and the biceps relaxes.

HOW HEAVY ARE MUSCLES?
Your muscles make up around one half of your body weight. Bones are much lighter—only around 14 percent of your total body weight.

INTERNET LINKS: www.kidshealth.org/kid/body/bones_SW.html

The body organs

The organs inside your body all work together to keep you alive and healthy. Your lungs help you breathe, your heart pumps blood around your body, and your brain controls every move that you make. Your liver, kidneys, stomach, and intestines process everything that you eat and drink.

Brain

Heart

Liver

Lung

Small intestine

Stomach

Large intestine

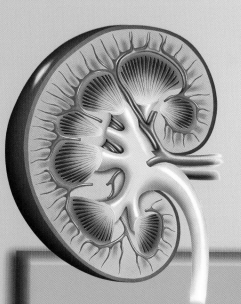

Cleaning up
You have two kidneys, and each one is around the size of your fist. Your kidneys filter blood, taking out unwanted water and chemicals. Urine is made from this waste and passed down to your bladder. You empty your bladder when you go to the bathroom.

▲ An organ is a part of your body that has a special job to do. Your body organs work hard all the time, even when you are asleep.

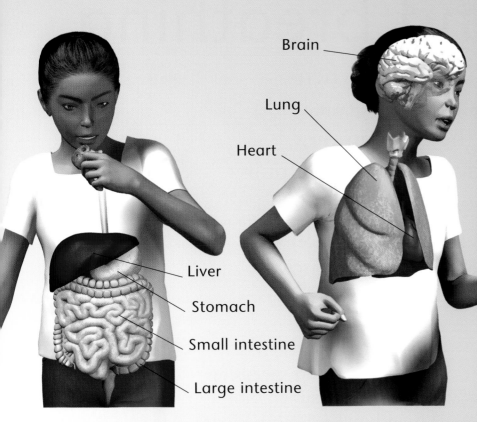

Brain

Lung

Heart

Liver

Stomach

Small intestine

Large intestine

◀ When you run, your brain tells your arms and legs to move, your lungs breathe in oxygen, and your heart pumps blood to your muscles.

▲ Your stomach and small intestine digest food. Your liver sorts chemicals and stores nutrients. Undigested food is held in the large intestine and is passed out of the body as waste.

CAN YOU FIND?
1. a brain
2. a lung
3. a heart
4. a liver
5. a stomach
6. a kidney
7. a small intestine
8. a large intestine

CREATIVE CORNER

Heart-rate experiment
Find your friend's pulse and feel it for one minute. Ask your friend to run around and then feel the pulse again. It will be faster than before. This is because the exercise has made your friend's heart beat faster.

Lungs and breathing

You never stop breathing, even when you are asleep. This is because your body needs oxygen, one of the gases in air. A strong muscle called the diaphragm pulls downward to make you breathe in. Air is sucked into your lungs. The lungs absorb oxygen, and then your diaphragm moves upward to make you breathe out again.

▼ When you blow up a balloon or blow out candles, you are breathing out a gas called carbon dioxide. This is a waste gas that your body does not need.

► When you exercise, your breathing speeds up. The extra oxygen that you breathe in is absorbed into your blood and pumped fast around your body.

Apache creation story

An Apache story from North America describes how the creator of all things made a small brown ball, around the size of a bean. He asked the wind to go inside the ball and blow it up. The ball became Earth, the planet that we now live on.

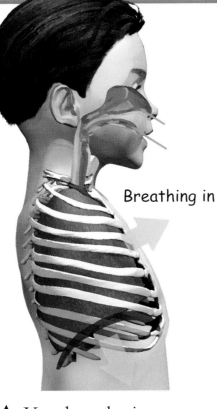

Breathing in

Breathing out

▲ You breathe in through your trachea, or windpipe. You can feel your chest expand as your lungs fill up with air.

▲ When you breathe out, you can feel your chest go down again. If your lungs were empty, they would collapse.

▲ You cannot breathe underwater because there is no oxygen. This is why scuba divers use oxygen tanks. Without the oxygen, they would die very quickly.

▲ Your breathing and heart rate slow down when you are sleeping. This usually happens around ten minutes after you have fallen asleep, when you begin to go into a deep sleep.

Inside your lungs

Air goes into each lung through a tube called a bronchus. The bronchus divides into many smaller tubes, which end in tiny stretchy sacs called alveoli. Oxygen passes through the alveoli into the blood, and carbon dioxide passes back through the alveoli into the lungs.

Group of alveoli

Heart and blood

The heart is a powerful muscle that pushes blood around your body. In one minute, the heart can pump a single drop of blood down to your toes and back up again. The blood is constantly moving around your body through long tubes called blood vessels. Blood carries oxygen from your lungs and nutrients from your food to all of your organs and muscles.

Largest artery (aorta)

  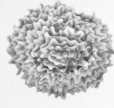

Red blood cell Platelet White blood cell

▲ One drop of blood contains millions of cells. Most of them are red, but some are white. Blood contains platelets, which help clots form. Blood cells and platelets float in a liquid called plasma.

Largest vein (vena cava)

Wall of muscle (septum)

The Tin Man
 In the story *The Wizard of Oz*, the Tin Man is sad because he is made of metal and has no heart. He goes in search of one, along with a scarecrow who needs a brain, a lion who needs courage, and a girl named Dorothy who needs to find her way home.

▲ The heart has two upper chambers and two lower chambers, divided in the middle by a wall of muscle. Blood flows in through veins and out through arteries.

VOCABULARY

cell

The smallest unit that there is of any living thing.

clot

Blood that thickens and sticks together, often to heal a wound to the body.

Upper chamber (atrium)

Lower chamber (ventricle)

▲ Exercise makes your heart stronger, helping it pump more blood with every heartbeat. This brings more oxygen to your muscles and body organs so that they can work better. It is important to exercise in order to keep your heart healthy.

◀ You have around 1 gal. (4L) of blood. Adults have more, and babies have less. You can give blood to help people who are sick or who have had serious accidents.

WHAT IS CIRCULATION?

Circulation is the movement of blood around your body. As your blood moves, it carries oxygen away from your lungs and brings back carbon dioxide.

Heart rate

Your heart rate is the number of times that your heart beats in one minute. Babies up to the age of one have a heart rate of 120–160 beats per minute. By the age of 12, this falls to around 70–80 beats per minute.

Food and digestion

The food that you eat takes a long journey through your body. The way that your body processes this food is called digestion. Some food is digested and turned into energy to keep your body active. Nutrients from the food help your body grow, stay healthy, and repair itself. Some food is not digested and is passed out of your body when you go to the bathroom.

▶ When your food reaches your stomach, it is churned up into a liquid. The liquid then flows through your small intestine. Nutrients from the food are passed into your blood and pumped around your body.

? HOW DO I SWALLOW?

When you swallow your food, strong muscles squeeze it throughout your digestive system. This process is called peristalsis.

▶ You get rid of undigested food when you go to the bathroom. When you were a baby, you had to wear a diaper to catch this waste.

Esophagus

Liver

Stomach

Small intestine

Large intestine

Fats keep you warm, but you need only a small amount. Eat fewer fats than other foods.

Foods that contain protein help your body heal itself, so eat plenty of protein.

Foods that are rich in carbohydrates give you energy and are important in your diet.

◀ Some foods are much better for you than others. This food pyramid shows the balance of the foods that you should eat to stay healthy. Avoid too many snacks that are full of fats and sugar.

Vitamins, minerals, and fiber keep your body healthy. You should eat plenty of fresh vegetables and fruit every day.

◀ Food gives you energy, and that energy is measured in calories. When you play sports, you use a lot of energy.

CREATIVE CORNER
Making a food poster
Divide a piece of paper into five sections. At the top of each section, write the name of a food group: grains, fruit and vegetables, dairy products, meats and proteins, and fats and sugars. Cut out some food pictures and stick them onto the correct section of your poster.

INTERNET LINKS: www.kidshealth.org/kid/body/digest_SW.html

Senses

You have five senses, and each one is important. Your senses help you experience the world around you and keep you safe by warning you about danger. You use your senses of sight and hearing to see and hear things. Smell and taste help you enjoy food, and you feel things with your sense of touch. Your brain controls all of your senses.

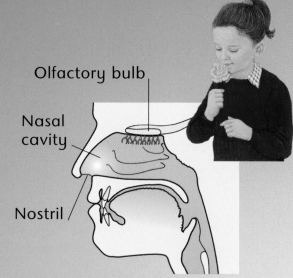

Olfactory bulb

Nasal cavity

Nostril

▲ Smell sensors in the olfactory (smelling) bulb in your nose send messages to your brain to tell you whether something, like a rose, smells good.

Reading by touch

Blind people use their sense of touch to read. Braille is an alphabet of raised dots that can be read by feeling them. It is named after its inventor, a Frenchman named Louis Braille.

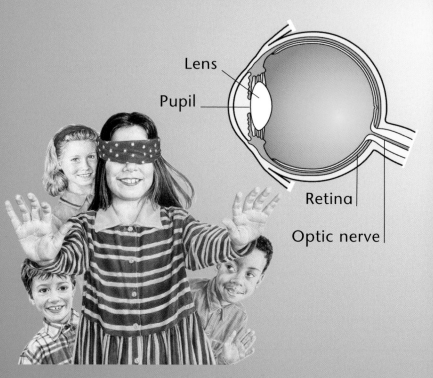

Lens

Pupil

Retina

Optic nerve

▲ You need your eyes to see. Light enters your eye through the pupil. An image is projected upside down onto the retina. Your brain turns this image around so that you see it the right way up.

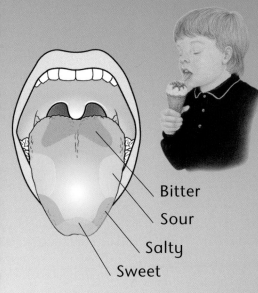

Bitter
Sour
Salty
Sweet

The emperor's new clothes

A silly emperor tells his people that he is wearing a fine robe, when he is really completely naked! Everyone believes him, except one boy. This boy trusts only what he can see with his own eyes and tells the emperor the truth.

▲ The tiny bumps on your tongue are called taste buds. Different areas of your tongue detect sweet, sour, salty, and bitter flavors.

► Waves of sound travel through the air to reach your ears. The loudness of a sound is measured in units called decibels. If you listen to a very loud sound for too long, you may damage your hearing.

Outer ear

Eardrum
Middle ear
Inner ear

Skin

Sensory nerve

Receptor cell at end of sensory nerve

◄ When you touch something, receptor cells under your skin send messages to your brain through sensory nerves. Your brain interprets these messages and makes you react to whatever you touch.

VOCABULARY

receptor cell
A cell that reacts to something by sending a message through the body to the brain.

optic nerve
This nerve takes messages from your eyes to your brain.

Brain and nerves

Your brain is one of the most important organs in your body. It is your body's control center. Your brain works by using a very complicated system of nerves. These nerves carry signals to and from your brain, reaching every single part of your body. The human brain looks a little like a wrinkled walnut. It has two halves called hemispheres, and each half controls different types of activities that the body carries out.

HOW BIG IS MY BRAIN?
Put your two fists together. Your brain is around that big. It is protected by a hard, bony case, which is called your skull.

Thought

Speech

▲ The left hemisphere of your brain controls all five senses. Your body sends signals to this part of your brain to process what you see, hear, touch, smell, and taste. The left side of your brain also controls thought, speech, and skilled movement.

Super brain
Your brain controls every action that you do. It helps you think, speak, feel emotions, and do many different things. Believe it or not, scientists think that most people use only around ten percent of their total brainpower!

Skilled
movement

Touch

Sight

Hearing, smell,
and taste

Brain stem

▲ If you touch something sharp, sensory nerves under your skin send messages to your brain.

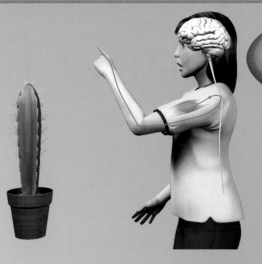

▲ Your brain reacts quickly, and you feel pain. Pain is a warning to stop doing something that hurts.

▼ Motorcyclists and bicyclists should always wear helmets. Helmets protect their delicate brains from injuries if they have an accident.

CREATIVE CORNER

The memory game

The left side of your brain helps you remember things. Ask a friend to put some objects onto a tray. Look at the objects and close your eyes while your friend takes one away. Can you remember which one is missing?

INTERNET LINKS: www.kidshealth.org/kid/body/brain_SW.html • http://faculty.washington.edu/chudler/neurok.html

A new life

Your amazing body is made up of billions of living units, which are called cells. But you began your life as one single cell, a fertilized egg inside your mother's body. You grew in her uterus, or womb, for around nine months, until you were ready to be born.

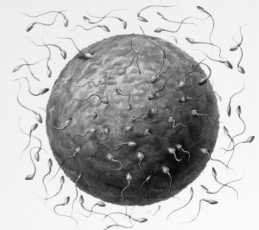

▲ Millions of sperm try to fertilize an egg, but only one will be successful. A new cell is created. This divides many times and slowly grows into a human baby.

◄ The fertilized egg travels to the mother's uterus and attaches itself. The new human life is called a fetus. At four weeks, it is around the size of your thumbnail.

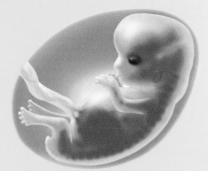

◄ The fetus grows, and after around eight weeks, it is around the size of your ear. It is already starting to look like a baby.

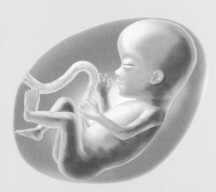

◄ The baby continues to grow inside a bag of watery liquid. A tube called the umbilical cord carries oxygen and nutrients from the mother to the baby. By 12 weeks, the baby is as big as your fist.

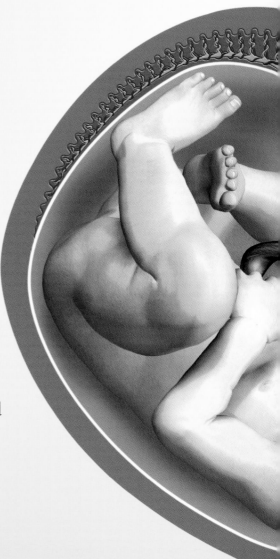

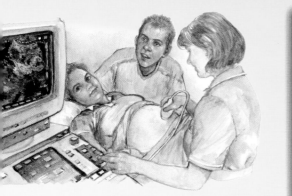

▲ A pregnant woman can see her baby when she has a sonogram. Doctors check that her baby is healthy and may tell her whether it is a boy or girl.

The founders of Rome
Romulus and Remus are twins in a famous Roman legend. Their mother abandoned them when they were babies, and a female wolf cared for them. Years later, they decided to start building the city of Rome, Italy, where the wolf had found them.

▼ There is not much space inside the uterus, so the growing baby lies with its arms and legs tucked up close to its body. After around 40 weeks, the baby leaves the womb, usually headfirst.

WHY DO I LOOK LIKE MY FAMILY?
Genes are the body's instructions for the creation of a new person, and parents pass them on to their children.

► When babies are first born, they sleep most of the time. They drink milk and do not eat solid food until they are around four to six months old.

INTERNET LINKS: www.kidshealth.org/kid/feeling/home_family/mom_pregnant.html

Growing older

As you get older, your body grows. During the first year after birth, the body grows very quickly. The growth is controlled by hormones, which are carried by your blood to different parts of your body. When you are an adult, you stop growing. Some old people get shorter as their bodies lose muscle and fat.

VOCABULARY

hormone
A substance that makes a part of your body react. Growth hormones make you grow.

teenager
A young person between the ages of 13 and 19 years old.

Growing pains
Have you ever wanted to grow to be as big as a giant or shrink to be as small as a mouse? In a famous children's story, a little girl named Alice drinks a potion that makes her become tiny and then eats a cake that makes her huge. These strange things happen in a place called Wonderland.

▲ By the time they are one year old, most babies have learned to crawl or walk.

► As children get older, they learn to control their muscles and hop, skip, and ride a bike. When they go to school, they learn how to read and write.

6 years old   12 years old   21 years old   65 years old

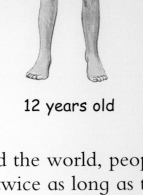

HOW FAST
WILL I GROW? **?**   219
Children grow at different
speeds, and by the age of ten,
some are taller than others.
They usually "catch up"
by the time they
are adults.

◄ Hormones make
you grow at particular
times—for example,
when you are a
teenager. They
also stop you from
growing when
you are around 21.

▼ Around the world, people
now live twice as long as they
did 200 years ago. It is
more common for
people to live to be
100 years old.

CREATIVE CORNER

Making a height chart

Draw a straight line on a
piece of paper. Write 20 in.
(50cm) at the bottom and mark
every 2 in. (5cm) up to
a 5-ft. (1.5-m) mark.
Draw a picture
next to the line.
Tape your
height chart
20 in. (50cm)
above ground
level and then
measure how
tall you are.

INTERNET LINKS: www.bbc.co.uk/science/humanbody/body/articles/lifecycle/teenagers/growth.shtml

Health and fitness

You must take care of your body to stay fit and healthy. If you neglect your body, you may become sick. It is important to make sure that you eat the right types of food and do not have too much fat or sugar in your diet. It is also very important to enjoy the things that you do. Stay active, and remember to exercise if you want to live a long, healthy, and happy life.

◄ Exercise keeps you healthy and is fun! Walk, run, and play sports as much as you can and get lots of fresh air.

The weight of the sky

In a Greek myth, superstrong Atlas fought against the gods of Mount Olympus. As a punishment for upsetting the gods, he was forced to stand at the edge of Earth and hold the weight of the sky on his shoulders. In pictures and statues of Atlas, the sky is often shown as a large sphere.

▲ To stay healthy, you need to bathe and brush your teeth regularly. Always wash your hands after you go to the bathroom.

VOCABULARY

physical
Having to do with the body and how all of the parts work together.

mental
Having to do with the mind and the way that the brain works.

◀ If you eat the right food, you are giving your body the nutrients that it needs to stay healthy and fight illness. You should eat at least five portions of fruit and vegetables every day as part of a healthy diet.

▼ It is good to hug the people you love because it makes you feel happy. Your emotional and mental health is very important, because it is linked to your physical health.

CREATIVE CORNER

Keeping a sleep diary

Did you sleep well last night? Keep a sleep diary for a few weeks. Write down how many hours of sleep you get each night. When you wake up each morning, make a note of how you feel. Do you think that there is a link between feeling good and sleeping well?

Fighting disease

If germs get inside your body, they multiply and cause an infection, which makes you sick. Your body is always fighting germs to keep you healthy. Sometimes you do not even know that this is happening. For example, when you cry, your tears are cleaning out the germs in your eyes.

▲ Sneezes and coughs are often symptoms of a common cold. You can take medicine to ease the symptoms of a cold, but there is no cure for the common-cold virus.

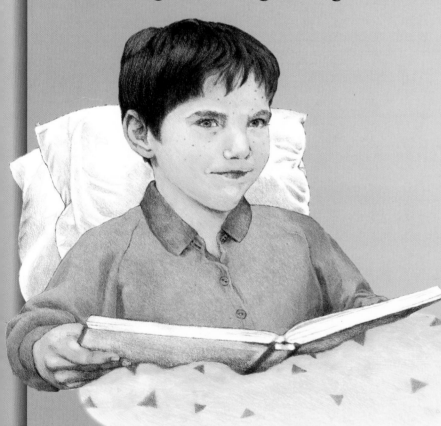

Pandora's box
Hermes, a Greek god, gave a box to Pandora, but told her never to open it. One day she felt curious and looked inside. Disease, Misery, and Death flew out, but then came Hope, to heal the sadness caused by the suffering.

▲ When you are sick, you may have a high body temperature. You may not have your usual amount of energy and need to rest in bed. You may feel very tired because your body is working hard to get better again.

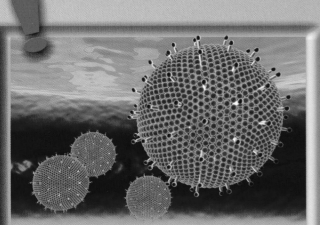

Vicious viruses

Some illnesses, such as chickenpox, are caused by viruses. Viruses live inside body cells and cannot be treated with antibiotics. Antiviral drugs may be used instead to stop viruses from reproducing inside the body.

▲ Medicines are also called drugs. They are made in different forms, including liquids, tablets, inhalers, and creams. Doctors prescribe different drugs for different health problems.

WHAT ARE ANTIBIOTICS?

Infections are caused by harmful bacteria. Antibiotics are chemicals that can attack and kill these bacteria.

▲ Babies and children are given vaccinations to stop them from getting some illnesses such as the measles and mumps. Some vaccinations are given as shots and others as pills or liquids.

▶ If you feel sick, you should visit your doctor. He or she will examine you to diagnose, or figure out, what is wrong with you.

Now you know!

► Your skeleton holds up your body and protects your organs. You were born with around 300 bones. Some fuse together as you grow.

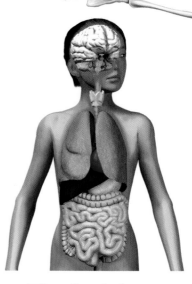

▲ You have five senses, which help you see, hear, smell, taste, and feel things. Your brain controls your senses.

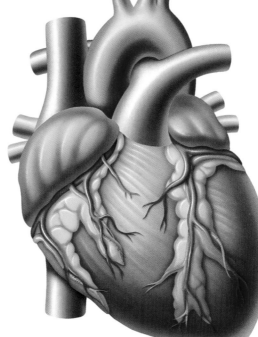

▲ The food that you eat is digested by your stomach and small intestine. Your large intestine stores the food that you do not need.

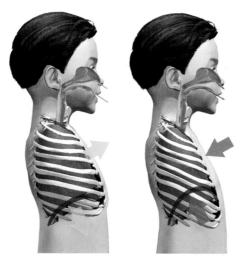

▲ Your heart is a muscle that pumps blood around your body. You need to stay in shape so that your heart can pump a lot of blood.

▲ You breathe oxygen in through your lungs. Your blood carries oxygen around your body. You breathe out carbon dioxide.

► Your brain is your body's control center. It works by using a complex system of nerves, carrying signals throughout your body.

Science

Science helps us answer questions about our world such as "What makes things start, go, and stop?" This chapter contains the answer to this question—and much more. It will help you make sense of your surroundings and understand why things happen in your everyday life.

What is science?

Science is all about how and why things happen in the world around us. It explains simple things, such as why a ball bounces, as well as more difficult ideas such as the speed of sound. Scientists try to answer questions by observing and experimenting to test their theories.

▼ Geologists study volcanoes by measuring the temperature and taking samples of the boiling-hot rocks. They find out what it is like deep inside Earth.

WHY IS SCIENCE IMPORTANT?
By studying our world, scientists find ways to increase our knowledge, improve our lives, and help people who are suffering.

▲ Scientific equipment includes many complicate machines. Among them a microscopes (above), which are used to look at things that are too small for the naked eye to see.

▲ One of the main branches of science is biology, the science of living things. Biologists study the bodies of plants and animals.

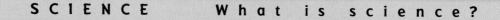

VOCABULARY
biology
The study of living things.
physics
The study of energy, forces, and matter.

Fibers

Fingerprint

Blood sample

Footprint

▶ When science is put to some type of practical use, such as building robots, this is called technology. Practical science like this is referred to as applied science.

▲ When scientists investigate a crime scene, they collect valuable clues. The evidence includes clothing fibers, samples of blood, and fingerprints.

▶ The oceans cover more than 70 percent of Earth's surface. Scientists need special equipment to survive there and carry out experiments.

▲ When you watch a fireworks display, you are watching the chemical energy in the fireworks as well as physics in action.

Materials

Materials, such as wood, metal, and glass, are the basic substances that everything is made from. There are hundreds of thousands of different materials, some of which are natural materials and some of which are human made. Materials have different properties that make them suitable for different purposes.

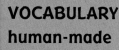

VOCABULARY
human-made
Describes artificial materials made by people.
properties
The characteristics of a particular material that affect the way that it behaves and how it is used by people.

◄ Some natural materials, such as wood, come from plants, and animals provide us with wool and leather. Others, such as stone, clay, and gold, are found in the ground.

► People use chemical processes to change raw materials, such as oil or sand, into new materials such as plastic.

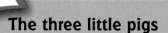

The three little pigs
Three little pigs build houses made out of different materials—straw, sticks, and bricks. A big, bad wolf blows down the flimsy straw and stick houses and eats two pigs. However, he cannot blow down the sturdy brick house.

► A skyscraper is built around a skeleton of strong steel rods and girders (beams). Skyscrapers need strong foundations, such as steel and concrete pillars, to support their weight.

CAN YOU FIND?
1. a man welding
2. a cage
3. a girder
4. a crane
5. a surveyor
6. a hardhat

◄ The Louvre pyramid in Paris, France, is made from one of the oldest human-made materials—glass. Glass is made by heating together sand, soda ash, and limestone.

CREATIVE CORNER

Making a stained-glass window

Draw a pattern of shapes on a piece of black paper. Cut out the shapes, leaving a frame around each one. Next, glue colored tissue paper behind the space in each frame. Tape the finished window to a real window so that the light shines through it.

Solids, liquids, and gase.

Everything around us is made from matter. The most common states, or types, of matter are solids, liquids, and gases. Most solids are hard and have a definite volume and shape. Liquids have a definite volume but no definite shape, while gases have no definite volume or shape.

► If you pour a liquid into a container, it takes on the shape of that container. When you boil liquid water, it changes into a gas called water vapor.

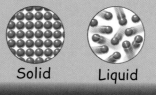

Solid	Liquid	Gas

▼ Rocks are typical solids. These columns of rocks formed from rivers of lava (below right) inside Earth. When the lava cooled down, it set into hard, solid shapes.

Aladdin and the genie
One day, a poor boy named Aladdin discovers that he can make a powerful genie appear by rubbing a magic lamp that supposedly has nothing but air inside it. The genie grants Aladdin's every wish. He becomes rich, marries the daughter of the sultan, and lives happily ever after.

WHAT IS OXYGEN?

Oxygen is a gas that has no color and does not smell. It makes up around one fifth of the atmosphere of Earth. We need to breathe in oxygen in order to stay alive.

▲ The most important gases on Earth are the mixture of gases in the air. Air moves faster over the top of an airplane's wings than it does underneath. This lifts the plane up into the air.

▼ Sounds are made when air moves back and forth very quickly, which is called a vibration. Big vibrations have a lot of energy and produce loud sounds.

Lava flow

CREATIVE CORNER

Air pressure

Fill a cup to the top with water. Now carefully slide a smooth piece of cardboard, such as a postcard, over the top. Hold your hand on the cardboard and slowly turn the cup upside down. Take away your hand, and the air pressure will keep the cardboard on the cup.

INTERNET LINKS: http://library.thinkquest.org/J001539/ • www.chem4kids.com/files/matter_intro.html

Mixing and reacting

Some substances, such as the salt and water in seawater, can be mixed together without changing chemically. This means that it is usually possible to separate mixtures into their different parts. When other substances come together, they break apart and change into new substances in a process called a chemical reaction. Baking a cake is a type of chemical reaction.

Burning
A common type of chemical reaction is burning. When substances burn, they combine with a gas called oxygen in the air and give out energy as heat and light. Fuels, such as coal and oil, burn well.

◄ Oil and water do not mix. Oil is lighter than water, so it floats on top. Oil sometimes spills from damaged oil tankers and is washed onto beaches. Sea birds with oily feathers cannot keep warm and dry.

CAN YOU FIND?
1. oily birds
2. oily seaweed
3. protective clothing
4. men digging

▲ In hot climates, salt can be separated from seawater. Heat from the sun makes the water disappear into the air, leaving the salt behind to be collected.

▶ When a cake is baked in the oven, there is a reaction. Bubbles of air and carbon-dioxide gas make the cake rise as it cooks.

▲ When you shake salad dressing, you make an emulsion. The oil breaks into little drops that "hang" in the vinegar. The same thing happens with peanut butter and mayonnaise.

CREATIVE CORNER

Fizzing volcano

Use modeling clay to shape a tall volcano with a large hole at the top. Spoon baking soda into the hole and mix in a few drops of red food coloring. Add some drops of vinegar and watch your volcano fizz as the vinegar and baking soda react, giving off bubbles of carbon dioxide.

INTERNET LINKS: www.chem4kids.com/files/react_intro.html

Energy

Energy makes things happen. It is invisible, but you can see, hear, and feel what it does to things around you. Energy can take many different forms such as heat, light, sound, and movement. All living things need energy to survive.

▲ Plants, such as sunflowers, use the energy in sunlight to make their own food. They use this energy to stay alive.

▼ You use up energy all the time, especially when you run around. You burn food inside your body to release energy.

▲ Energy is never made or lost. When this pole-vaulter jumps, the chemical energy stored in his muscles changes into movement and heat energy.

Power and energy

The world's supplies of oil and gas will probably last for around another 70 years. The energy that we get from these natural resources will then not be available. New oil and gas reserves may be discovered in the future. We do not know how quickly we will use up any newly found resources.

▶ The wind turns the blades of these wind turbines and the movement energy is turned into electricity. Wind farms do not cause pollution.

Making cars move

The gasoline that we put into our cars gives them the energy to move. When the gas burns in the car engine, the stored energy is released.

► The solar panels on the Hubble telescope capture the Sun's energy and turn it into electricity. This is used to run the computers and scientific equipment that keep the telescope working.

► Nuclear power plants use the energy given out by natural radioactive materials when their atoms split. This produces heat, which is then used to turn water into steam and to generate electricity.

INTERNET LINKS: www.eia.doe.gov/kids/energyfacts/science/formsofenergy.html

Heat and temperature

Heat is a form of movement energy, because the hotter something gets, the faster its particles move. Heat is the energy that something has because its particles are moving. A temperature scale measures heat energy and tells us how hot something is.

▶ The air inside a hot-air balloon is heated with a gas flame. The heat makes the particles in the air move farther apart and become less dense, or lighter, than the air outside the balloon. This is why the balloon rises up into the sky.

VOCABULARY
thermometer
A device for measuring how hot or cold something is.
Fahrenheit scale
A temperature scale on which water freezes at 32° and boils at 212°.

Melting wings

A Greek myth tells how Daedalus and his son Icarus tried to escape from the island of Crete. Daedalus made wings from feathers glued with wax. Icarus flew too close to the sun. The heat melted the wax, and he fell into the sea and drowned.

Thermometer in the winter

Thermometer in the summer

◀ We measure temperature with a thermometer. When the temperature rises, the mercury or colored alcohol expands and rises up the tube.

Rainforest people

Native Americans in Canada

◀ In places with cold winters, people need warmer clothes and homes than people living in rainforests, where it is hot all year round.

▶ We cannot usually see heat, but if objects are heated to very high temperatures (such as in a fire), they glow red or white. They are giving off light energy, which we can see.

HOW DOES HEAT TRAVEL?

In a liquid or a gas, heat is carried by the movement of the liquid or gas. This is called convection. Conduction is when, in a solid, heat spreads from particle to particle.

▲ The heat from a campfire helps us stay warm. Several layers of clothes keep us warmer than one item of thick clothing. This is because air is trapped between the layers and does not let body heat pass through easily.

INTERNET LINKS: www.exploratorium.edu/snacks/iconheat.html • www.chem4kids.com/files/react_thermo.html

Changing states

Most substances will change from one state of matter to another when the temperature or pressure changes. As temperatures rise, solids melt into liquids and liquids boil into gases. As temperatures fall, liquids freeze into solids and gases turn back into liquids.

▼ Water is an unusual substance because it exists as a solid, a liquid, and a gas in everyday life. It often changes its state. Liquid water changes into solid ice when it is frozen.

? WHAT IS CONDENSATION?
This is the process by which a gas cools down and turns into a liquid. As the gas cools, the particles move closer together, which makes the gas turn into a liquid.

▲ When we boil water in a teakettle, bubbles of gas form in the liquid and escape up the spout. This process is called evaporation.

▲ Pipes often burst in freezing weather. This is because water expands when it freezes solid and pushes against the pipes, causing cracks to form. The liquid water pours out of the cracks.

▲ The metal used to build bridges changes size when it is heated or cooled by the weather. As the metal heats up, it expands. As the metal cools down, it contracts.

◄ Many solids and gases can dissolve in liquids and become part of the liquids. In soda, the bubbles are carbon-dioxide gas that has been forced into the liquid drink under pressure.

▲ When you heat popcorn kernels, the air inside them grows bigger, or expands. The outsides split, and the kernels explode with a pop.

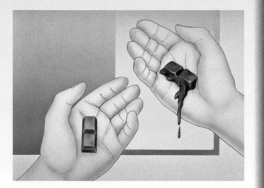

CREATIVE CORNER

Making an ice balloon

Fill a balloon with cold water and tie the neck. Put it inside a large plastic bag and leave it in the freezer overnight. The next morning, use scissors to cut away the balloon from the ice. Float the ice in a bowl of water. How much of the ice balloon is below the surface?

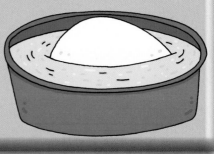

▲ The heat from your hands makes the particles in chocolate move freely over one another. This makes the chocolate melt.

INTERNET LINKS: www.bbc.co.uk/schools/scienceclips/ages/8_9/solid_liquids.shtml

Electricity

Without electricity, our lives would be very different. There would be no electric lights, and machines such as computers, cars, and toasters would not work. Electricity is a very useful form of energy. It can be easily changed into light or heat.

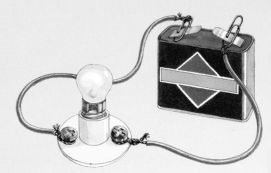

▲ Electricity flows along a wire in a path called a circuit. Here, the bulb lights up when electricity stored in the battery travels along the wire.

▼ A virtual-reality helmet allows this boy to enter a world created by a computer. He can press buttons on the glove to change the images that he sees.

▼ Electric toasters have timers, which make the bread pop up when it has cooked for a set time. This usually stops us from burning our toast!

Frankenstein's monster
In a story by Mary Shelley, Frankenstein creates an artificial man by attaching together pieces of dead bodies. In movies, he brings his monster to life with the power of a huge lightning flash during a big electrical storm.

Cars need the electricity in their batteries in order to work. Electric sparks make the gasoline burn inside the engine, and this makes the car move.

HOW HOT IS LIGHTNING?

Lightning heats up the air to very high temperatures—as much as five times as hot as the surface of the Sun! This makes the air suddenly expand, producing thunder.

▲ Static electricity is made by rubbing things together. If you rub a balloon against your hair, it gives it a static-electric charge, which pulls your hair and makes it stand on end.

VOCABULARY

circuit
A pathway along which electricity flows.

static electricity
A form of electricity produced by rubbing things together. It can produce positive or negative charges.

▶ Lightning is a huge spark of static electricity that builds up inside storm clouds. When the electricity jumps down to the ground, it releases energy.

Magnets

Magnets are pieces of metal or stone that are surrounded by an invisible force. They may pull things toward them (attract them) or push them away (repel them). Magnets occur naturally in rocks in the ground, but some materials, such as iron, can be made into magnets.

▲ Earth is like a giant magnet. Migrating birds are able to sense this magnetism. They use it to stay on course during long journeys.

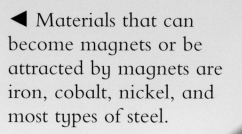

◄ Materials that can become magnets or be attracted by magnets are iron, cobalt, nickel, and most types of steel.

WHAT ARE ELECTROMAGNETS?

Some materials act like magnets only when electricity is passed through them. When the electricity is turned off, they stop being magnetic.

Lodestones

Around 1,000 years ago, people noticed that certain rocks pointed north and south when they were allowed to swing freely. Sailors used these "leading stones," or lodestones, to find their way across oceans. The later name "magnet" comes from Magnesia, in modern-day Turkey.

Magnetic guide

A compass needle is a tiny magnet. The needle always swings to point north–south because it is pulled by the strong magnetic forces inside Earth.

▼ A maglev (magnetic levitation) train and the track that it runs on have electromagnets on them. The two magnets repel, or push each other apart. This means that the train "floats" above the track.

▼ In a bicycle dynamo, a magnet moves as the wheel turns and produces electricity, which makes the bicycle light work.

◀ Electromagnets are used to pick up heavy scrap iron and move it around. When the electricity is turned off, the iron falls.

CREATIVE CORNER

Making a compass

Stroke a needle several times with one end of a magnet in one direction. Now put some water into a saucer and float a piece of cork on the surface. Put the needle on top of the cork. The needle will turn to point north–south.

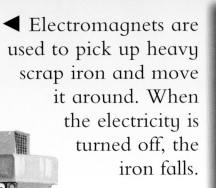

Forces

Forces are the pushes and pulls that get things moving and change the way that they move. Forces can make things speed up, slow down, or change direction, size, or shape. Contact forces, such as kicking a ball, need objects to be touching. When energy is used, forces are involved.

Force of gravity

A pendulum is a weight that hangs from a fixed point and swings from side to side under the action of gravity. Gravity pulls things on Earth down toward the ground.

▲ We cannot see pushing and pulling forces, but we can see the effect that they have on things around us. This miner feels his muscles getting tired as he uses up stored energy by pushing.

◄ The arrows on this tugboat and these barges show that when there is a force acting on something in one direction, the object applies an equal force in the opposite direction.

Tug of war

An African myth tells how a clever hare bet a big elephant that he could beat him in a tug of war. Then he hid behind some bushes and made the same bet with a hippo. Each thought that he was competing with the hare.

▲ A rubbing force called friction will try to stop moving objects. A bowling ball and its lane are smooth, so there is little friction.

▼ Motorcyles on a "wall of death" keep going around and around because a force called centripetal force pulls them in toward the center.

▶ In pool, the push of the cue makes the first ball move. The second ball moves only when it is pushed.

?

HOW ARE FORCES MEASURED?
The strength of a force is measured in newtons (N), after English scientist Sir Isaac Newton. One newton is around the force it takes to lift an empty glass.

▲ The shape of a rowboat helps it move faster. It cuts down the amount of resistance, or drag, caused by the water rubbing against the boat.

▶ Hot gases shoot backward out of rocket engines. This produces an equal force in the opposite direction, and the rocket shoots upward.

Floating and sinking

If you try to push a tennis ball under the water in a bowl and then let go, the water pushes the ball back to the surface. This upward push is called upthrust. An object will float if the upthrust is equal to its weight. It will sink if its weight is greater than the upthrust.

Salty sea
The very salty water in the Dead Sea is much denser than ordinary seawater. It pushes up more strongly against objects, helping them float. This is why it is so easy to float there.

▲ Small objects made from different materials act differently in a bowl of water. Metal objects sink, while cork, wood, and plastic float.

◀ The arm bands that this girl is wearing are full of air. They help her float because air is less dense than water.

▼ Our bodies have a lot of air inside them and are less dense than water. This is why we float. These divers wear heavy weights on their belts to resist the upthrust of the water.

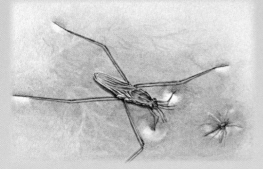

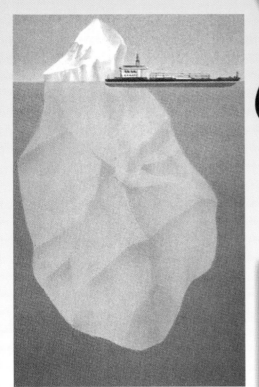

▲ The long legs of this pond skater spread its weight. It can walk over the stretchy "skin" on the surface of the water without sinking. Its feet make little dips but do not break through.

? **HOW DOES A BIG SHIP FLOAT?**
A big ship will float because it is hollow. The water that the ship pushes out of the way creates an upthrust that balances the downward force of the ship's weight.

▲ After long periods of heavy rain, rivers burst their banks and flood dry land. People make rafts out of anything that will float!

▲ Submarines have special tanks that can be filled with either air or water. To dive, water is let into the tanks, making the submarine heavy enough to sink.

▲ Ice is slightly less dense than water, which means that it can float on water. Most of the huge floating blocks of ice called icebergs are under the water.

CREATIVE CORNER

Testing for surface tension
Pour some milk into a shallow dish. Add a few drops of food coloring. They will float on the surface, not breaking through the "skin" of the milk. Now add some dish soap to break the skin and let the colors spread.

INTERNET LINKS: www.kids-science-experiments.com/cat_floating.html

Gravity and weight

An invisible pulling force called gravity attracts objects to one another. It is most obvious when one of the objects is much larger than the other. Earth is a huge planet, and its gravity pulls all of the objects on the planet down to the ground. If Earth did not have gravity, objects would not weigh anything.

▲ The scientist Sir Isaac Newton thought about gravity when he saw an apple fall from a tree. He said that Earth's gravity could also pull the Moon and keep it circling around Earth.

► When we weigh apples, we are really measuring what they are made of. To a scientist, the word for this is *mass*, and it is measured in ounces or grams.

WHAT DOES THE SUN'S GRAVITY DO?

The huge pull of the Sun's gravity holds Earth and all of the other planets in our solar system in place. It keeps them circling around the Sun.

▲ To lift and balance these weights, the boy has to push upward with a strong force to overcome the downward pull of gravity. When he holds steady, the forces inside and outside are evenly balanced.

▲ The Moon is smaller than Earth. It has only one sixth of the gravitational pull. Astronauts can jump six times higher on the Moon than on Earth because there is less gravity pulling them down.

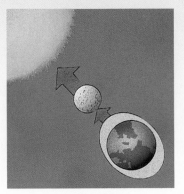

High tide

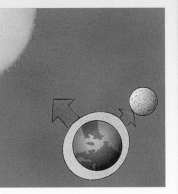

Low tide

▲ The pull of the Moon's gravity tugs at Earth's oceans, making them rise and fall as the Moon circles Earth. At high tide the sea rises and at low tide it falls.

The center of gravity

In any object, the point at which the effect of gravity seems to be concentrated is called the center of gravity or center of balance. In an object with a regular shape, the center of gravity is in the middle. Your center of gravity is in the middle of your chest. If an object is supported directly below its center of gravity, it will balance. It is easier to balance an object if it has a low center of gravity. A racecar has a low center of gravity.

INTERNET LINKS: www.kids-science-experiments.com/cat_gravity.html

Light and color

Light is a form of energy that travels faster than anything else. The Sun produces most of the natural light on Earth as a result of nuclear reactions. A few animals, such as fireflies and deep-sea fish, produce natural light using chemical reactions inside their bodies. People produce artificial light in electric light bulbs.

Primary colors
Red, green, and blue are the primary colors of light. You can mix them together to make almost any other color. If red, green, and blue lights are mixed, we see them as white (ordinary) light.

Rainbow colors in a drop of water

► Sunlight and electric light appear white but are actually made up of all of the colors of the rainbow. The spray of water from a hose makes the colors spread out, so you can see each one.

Rainbow route
An African legend tells how all of the creatures on Earth were stolen from the sky god and creator, Amma, by the Dagon. A male and female of each animal in heaven and a sample of every plant were placed in a giant pyramid, which slid down to Earth on a rainbow.

◀ The Sun makes its own light, and this takes only eight minutes to reach Earth. The Moon cannot make its own light. It can shine only when it reflects light from the Sun down onto Earth.

The Sun at sunset

Candle

▶ Burning a candle uses up the stored energy in the wax, which is a type of fuel. In a light bulb, electrical energy makes a wire so hot that it glows with a bright light.

The Moon at night

Electric light bulb

▶ Light travels in straight lines and cannot bend around objects. If something, such as a large rock, blocks the light, a shadow forms behind it. It is much cooler in shadows.

▲ Travelers in a desert sometimes think that they see a pool of water. This is a mirage. What they see is really a reflection of the sky.

CREATIVE CORNER

Making a rainbow disk
On a circle of white cardboard, color six equal sections in order: red, orange, yellow, green, blue, and purple. Push a small, sharp pencil through the middle of the cardboard. Spin the disk fast. It will look white.

INTERNET LINKS: www.physics4kids.com/files/light_intro.html

Sound

Sound is a form of energy made by something moving rapidly back and forth (vibrating). It passes on the vibrations in the form of a traveling wave. Sound waves travel through solids, liquids, and gases, but they cannot travel through space because there are no particles to vibrate.

Making sounds louder

Sound waves spread out like ripples from a stone thrown into a pond. Using a megaphone will make sounds louder because the sounds are trapped inside the cone, instead of spreading out into the air.

◀ Animals cannot see sounds. Instead, they can pick up the vibrations through their ears.

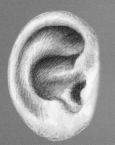

Humans have external ears.

Bats have large external ears.

Crickets have ears on their knees.

Frogs have eardrums on the sides of the head.

▶ Musical instruments make sounds by causing something to vibrate. This can be the strings on a violin or the air in the pipe of a recorder or trumpet. High notes come from rapid vibrations and low notes come from slower vibrations.

▶ Supersonic aircraft fly faster than the speed of sound. As the aircraft overtakes its own sound, it breaks through the sound barrier and makes a loud bang called a sonic boom.

A dolphin using echoes

A ship using echoes

▲ Sound waves bouncing back from surfaces are called echoes. They can be used to find the positions of objects by timing how long the echo takes to return.

▶ Microphones can be used to record the sounds of a journalist's voice. They turn sound waves into electrical signals.

CREATIVE CORNER

Bottle music

Collect several small glass bottles, all the same size and shape. Place them in a line and fill each bottle with a different amount of water. Blow gently across the tops of the bottles and compare the different notes that they give out. Which bottles make high notes and which make low notes?

INTERNET LINKS: www.howstuffworks.com/hearing.htm

Changing our lives

Science helps us understand how our lives are changing the future of the planet. We are polluting the air, land, and water with our waste materials. Science can help us care for our world and make it a better place to live in the future.

Global warming
The world is getting warmer at a faster rate than it would naturally because of polluting gases. These gases trap some of the heat given off by Earth so that it cannot escape into space.

▼ Most forms of transportation have a bad effect on the environment. Building airplanes, cars, ships, and trains uses up energy and raw materials. These vehicles also use up energy in the form of fuel and pollute the air with fumes.

▶ From paper and plastic to bottles and cans, all types of materials can be recycled. This saves us from using new raw materials, cuts down on the energy used, and reduces pollution.

WHAT IS A CARBON FOOTPRINT?
This is the amount of carbon dioxide produced by the burning of fossil fuels (coal, oil, and gas) over the course of one year.

▲ Planting trees helps soak up a lot of carbon dioxide, because all plants use carbon dioxide to make their own food.

▲ Biosphere 2 is an enormous greenhouse in Arizona. It was built to test ways of managing ecosystems on Earth.

▲ Most whales are threatened by pollution and oil exploration in the oceans. They also suffer owing to the noise from, and collisions with, ships, as well as the danger of becoming trapped in fishnets.

CREATIVE CORNER

Collage of recycled materials

Collect small pieces of different types of materials that would be thrown away such as shiny paper, plastic containers, wooden strips, and sticks. Use the recycled materials to make a collage showing a city of the future growing out of a garbage dump.

Now you know!

▲ Natural materials, such as clay and wood, come from plants or animals or are found in the ground.

▲ Baking a cake is a type of chemical reaction. As the cake bakes, the ingredients break apart and change into new substances.

▲ The most common states of matter are solids, liquids, and gases. Water can be a liquid, a solid (ice), or a gas (water vapor).

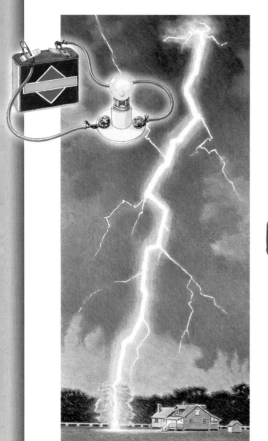

▲ Drops of water make the colors in light spread out so that you can see each color by itself.

▲ When one thing moves over another, a force called friction tries to stop the movement.

▲ Current electricity flows along wires in a path called a circuit. Static electricity is produced by rubbing things together.

▶ Musical instruments make sounds by making the air vibrate, or shake back and forth. High notes come from fast vibrations and low notes from slow vibrations.

Space

How big is our universe? How long has space been there? People have wondered about questions like these for at least as long as we have had historical records. Today it seems as though we are merely beginning to find out just how enormous—and how complicated—space really is.

Our universe

The universe means everything that exists. It includes Earth and all of the other planets, hundreds of billions of stars, and all of space. It is bigger than we can possibly imagine. People have studied the universe since ancient times, and slowly we are beginning to understand how it works.

◄ The *Saturn V* rocket powered the *Apollo 11* mission in 1969. This was the first mission to land astronauts on the Moon.

5. Around one billion years later, galaxies form

4. 300,000 years later, the universe fills with light

Vishnu and the universe
In the Hindu religion, Vishnu is the god who protects the universe. When it is at peace, he sleeps on the snakelike coils of another divine being, Sesha. When there is disorder, Vishnu battles it himself or sends a helper to restore peace.

6. The universe today

WHAT IS GRAVITY?

Gravity is the force that keeps everything, including people, on the surface of Earth. It also holds all of the universe together.

▲ In 1929, astronomer Edwin Hubble proved that the universe is expanding, which helped confirm the big bang theory. The Hubble space telescope is named after him.

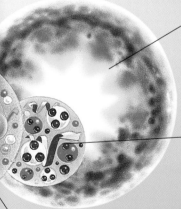

1. The big bang happens, 14 billion years ago

2. Seconds later, the first particles form

3. Minutes later, gas particles form

▲ Scientists believe that the universe was formed in a huge explosion, known as the "big bang."

CREATIVE CORNER

Making a model rocket

Cut slits in the top of a cardboard tube and overlap the tabs to make a narrow neck. Add triangular fins at the bottom. Cut a slit from the edge to the middle of a circle of cardboard to form the nose cone and add it to the top of your rocket.

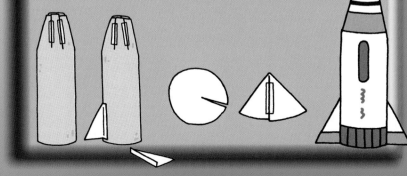

The Sun

The Sun is a star and the center of our solar system. It is an enormous ball of burning gases, millions of times bigger than Earth. The Sun sends out heat and light. Without these things, it would not be possible for plants and animals to live on Earth.

▶ The core, or middle, of the Sun is its hottest part. Hot gases bubble up to the surface. There, they form a halo of gases called a corona. There are dark patches on the surface, which are cooler. They are called sunspots.

Sunspot _____

▲ Roosters will often crow at the start of the day when, as we say, "the Sun rises." But the Sun does not really rise at all. In fact, day begins when the part of Earth where you are spins to face the Sun.

How Kuat the sun god brought daylight
In Brazil, there is a story about the Mamaiurans, Amazon Indians who were forced to live in darkness because the wings of the birds blocked the sky. Kuat kidnapped the vulture king and forced him to agree to share daylight. This is why there is day and night.

Core

Corona

Solar eclipse

When the Moon passes between Earth and the Sun, it causes a solar eclipse. During a complete solar eclipse, the Moon's shadow covers the entire face of the Sun for a few minutes. The corona of the Sun, which we normally cannot see, becomes visible.

▼ Sometimes there are violent explosions on the Sun, and streams of electrically charged particles shoot up from the surface. These are called solar flares. Most of them happen around sunspots.

◄ In some places, the Sun may be seen for 24 hours each day. In the most northern part of Norway, the Sun does not set for 76 days from May through July.

The solar system

When we refer to the solar system, we mean the Sun and everything that orbits, or circles, it. This includes the planets, their moons, comets, meteors, and asteroids. All of these things are held close to the Sun by its very strong gravity.

▶ Stars and planets are formed from gas and dust. Our solar system includes our Sun, which is a star, and the planets that orbit it. The Sun formed and began to shine around five billion years ago. Then, more than 500 million years ago, the planets formed around it.

Neptune

Uranus

Saturn

Ancient gods
Besides Earth, the planets in the solar system are named after ancient gods. Jupiter was the father of the Roman gods. Other planets named after Roman gods are Mars, the god of war; Mercury, the messenger of the gods; Venus, the goddess of love; Saturn, the god of the harvest; and Neptune, the god of the sea. Uranus was the ancient Greek god of the sky.

Sun

Copernicus

Nicolaus Copernicus was the first person to suggest, in 1543, that Earth and the other planets revolve around the Sun. Before he made this claim, people believed that Earth was at the center of the universe.

Mercury

Venus

Earth

Mars

Jupiter

CREATIVE CORNER

A memory game

Draw a picture of each of the eight planets in the solar system on two sets of index cards and label them. Shuffle and lay the cards face-down on a table. Take turns to turn over two cards. If they match, keep the pair and have another turn. The person with the most pairs wins the game.

Galaxies

A galaxy is a cluster, or island, of stars in space. Our Sun is one of hundreds of billions of stars in our particular galaxy, which is the Milky Way. All of the stars that we can see in the sky belong to the Milky Way. Our galaxy is only one of billions of galaxies that make up the universe.

WHAT MAKES A GALAXY'S SHAPE?
All galaxies are held together by gravity, but scientists do not yet know what makes them a particular shape.

◀ There is a lot of gas and dust between the planets. We notice this only when sunlight reflects off the gas and dust. This makes the particles glow in the sky.

Illapa and the Milky Way
The ancient South American people, the Inca, believed in a thunder god named Illapa. He was said to gather water from the Milky Way and store it inside a jug. When it rained, people said that Illapa had broken the jug with a stone shot from his sling.

▶ The Milky Way is a spiral galaxy. Its central area contains many old stars, which give it a yellow-red glow. The younger stars in the spiral arms of the galaxy burn brighter, and they have a blue-white light.

Types of galaxies

▶ Elliptical galaxies are almost egg shaped. Some of the largest galaxies are ellipticals.

▶ Spiral galaxies have a central core and curved "arms." The stars in the arms orbit the galactic center.

▶ Galaxies that cannot be described as either of the above types are called irregular.

Elliptical galaxy

Spiral galaxy

Irregular galaxy

CREATIVE CORNER

Making a galaxy greeting card

Fold a piece of cardboard or thick paper in half. Paint the front dark blue or black, for the night sky. Using clear glue, draw some curvy, swirly shapes. Sprinkle glitter or salt over all. Then shake off the excess to see your own galaxy!

INTERNET LINKS: www.esa.int/esaKIDSen/Starsandgalaxies.html • www.frontiernet.net/~kidpower/galaxies.html

Rocky planets

Of the eight planets that orbit the Sun, four are called "rocky planets." These are the four planets that are the closest to the Sun: Mercury, Venus, Earth, and Mars. The four rocky planets are much smaller than the four "gas giants" that are farthest from the Sun.

HOW DID THEY FORM?
The rocky planets began as dust and gas. Over time, they grew, gathering dust and gas, until, finally, they became planets.

▶ Venus is almost the same size as Earth, but is closer to the Sun. It is covered in thick, poisonous clouds, and its surface is hot, at around 890°F (475°C).

Venus

Ferry man
Charon, the name of Pluto's neighbor, was the ferry man of the dead in ancient Greek mythology. Charon had close links to Hades, the god of the underworld, who was renamed Pluto by the Romans.

▼ Mercury is the planet that is the closest to the Sun. It has no protective atmosphere. This means that the surface facing the Sun is extremely hot, while the surface facing away from the Sun is extremely cold.

▼ Earth is the only planet known to support life. It is not too hot or too cold. It also has water and oxygen, both of which are needed for life.

Pluto and Charon

Until recently, Pluto (below, bottom) was believed to be a planet. But scientists have recently decided that it does not qualify as one, and it is no longer counted among the planets in the solar system. Pluto is now called a dwarf planet along with its neighbor, Charon (at left, top).

Earth

Mars

◄ Mars has similar features to those on Earth such as valleys, mountains, and polar icecaps. It is possible that at one time Mars was also home to a form of life.

VOCABULARY

atmosphere
A layer of gases around a planet. Earth's atmosphere provides the air that we breathe.

polar
At the far north or south end of a planet.

INTERNET LINKS: www.esa.int/esaKIDSen/SEMF8WVLWFE_OurUniverse_0.html

Gas giants

The four planets that are farthest from the Sun—Jupiter, Saturn, Uranus, and Neptune—are known as the gas giants. They have only a small, rocky core, which is surrounded by gas and liquid. All four have rings and moons, and impressive storms can happen in their atmospheres.

▲ William Herschel discovered Uranus in 1781. It was the first planet to be identified using a telescope.

◄ Saturn is almost as big as Jupiter, and it has the most moons. Scientists have named 35 of them.

Viking Valhalla
Early peoples often believed that the gods lived in the sky. The Vikings thought that the souls of warriors who had fought bravely and died in battle would go to Valhalla. This was a big hall in the sky where they would feast and be happy forever.

▶ Jupiter is the biggest planet of all and spins the fastest. It has 16 moons, and swirling gas clouds cover its surface.

▶ Uranus has 21 moons and faint rings. Its blue-green color is probably caused by methane gas in its atmosphere.

◀ Neptune, the planet that is farthest from the Sun, is a very cold, dark place. It has three rings, eight moons, and the stormiest weather of all of the planets in the solar system.

CREATIVE CORNER

A mobile of Saturn and its rings

Make two half planets out of papier-mâché. When they are dry, trim the edges so that the pieces fit together and then paint them yellow. Take a large paper plate and paint it with dark and light rings. Thread a knotted piece of string through the center of all three pieces to hang up your mobile!

Earth and Moon

Our planet, Earth, is the only planet on which we know that there is life. From space, a lot of Earth looks blue. This is because three fourths of its surface is covered by water. This water, the air in the atmosphere, and the planet's temperature are what allow life on Earth to exist.

▶ Most astronomers believe that the Moon and Earth formed around 4.5 million years ago from a cloud of dust and gas.

Shape-changing Moon

Earth has only one moon. At night, it often seems to glow with its own light. In fact, this light is reflected sunlight. As the Moon orbits Earth, we see different phases, or shapes, of the Moon. This depends on how much of the sunlit side of the Moon we can see from Earth.

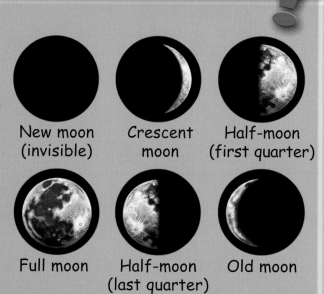

New moon
(invisible)

Crescent
moon

Half-moon
(first quarter)

Full moon

Half-moon
(last quarter)

Old moon

Walking on the Moon

Apollo 14 was the eighth manned *Apollo* mission and the third to land on the Moon. Two crew members walked on the surface, and one even hit a golf ball. This mission brought back almost 93 lbs. (42kg) of samples from the surface.

Low tide

High tide

▲ Tides are caused by the Moon's gravity as it orbits Earth. It pulls the water toward it, causing high tides. The Moon also pulls Earth toward it, making the water rise on the other side of Earth and causing low tides.

CREATIVE CORNER

Keeping a Moon diary

Take a sheet of paper and divide it into seven columns. Label each column with a day of the week. Every evening for a month, draw the moon shape that you see in the box in its column. You will soon see a pattern in the shapes.

MON	TUE	WED	THU	FRI	SAT	SUN
☽	☽	☽	☽	☽	☽	☽
○	○	○	○	○	○	○
○	○	◑	◑	◑	◑	◑
◖	◖	◖				

Asteroids and comets

Asteroids and comets are small, rocky bodies that orbit the Sun. However, their gravity is not strong enough to pull them into a spherical shape like the planets. Meteors are pieces of rock, up to around the size of a baseball, that have broken off comets or asteroids. We see them in the sky as "shooting stars."

◄ Comets have long, oval-shaped orbits. They are "active" and glowing when they are close to the Sun. This is when we can see them, often for several days at a time.

Pahokatawa

A Native American people, the Pawnee, had a story about a man named Pahokatawa, who was killed and eaten by wild animals. He was brought back to life by the gods and returned to Earth as a meteor.

▲ Most asteroids are found between Mars and Jupiter, in an area called the asteroid belt.

▼ Comets have two tails. The gas tail points away from the Sun and looks bluish. The dust tail is often curved and glows white.

Meteorites
When a meteor falls to Earth, it is called a meteorite. Around 500 meteorites reach Earth each year. We hardly notice most of them, but sometimes a large meteorite can cause a lot of damage. This crater in Arizona was caused by a meteorite.

CAN YOU FIND?
1. a comet
2. an asteroid
3. a crater
4. two astronomers
5. the Moon

INTERNET LINKS: http://library.thinkquest.org/3645/comets.html • www.kidsastronomy.com/asteroid.htm

1. A star forms
inside a nebula

2. Gas and
dust condense

Life of a star

Stars are formed out of dust and gas and grow larger as they get older. They burn brightly for a while, but then begin to run out of gases to burn. Gradually, they collapse and die. When a star dies, it creates dust and gas that may become part of another star.

Iroquois stars

An ancient story from an Iroquois tribe of North America tells of people who behaved so badly that the Sun and the Moon left. Some children floated up to the sky with fires and became stars. The Sun and the Moon were so pleased that they returned.

▲ When they die, very big stars collapse into black holes. The gravity of a black hole is so strong that it sucks in everything close to it, including light.

3. The dust-and-gas cloud grows

4. Gases fuse and release heat and light

5. A new star begins to shine

▲ A star forms in a nebula, where dust and gas condense (squash together) and attract more dust and gas. As the cloud grows, hydrogen gas atoms fuse (join together) to form helium. This releases heat and light, and the star begins to shine.

Supernova

A supernova happens just before a neutron (big, collapsed) star or a black hole forms. When a dying star explodes, it burns brightly for a few weeks or months. During this time, it makes as much energy as our Sun would in ten billion years!

▶ The Horsehead nebula is found in the constellation, or group of stars, known as Orion. Dark clouds like this one are the parts of nebulae in which new stars form.

Looking into space

People have been fascinated by the stars since ancient times. Early civilizations, including the Sumerians, Babylonians, and Egyptians, spent a lot of time studying the sky and how it changed over time. The ancient Greeks learned a lot from earlier societies and made huge advances in astronomy—the study of the universe.

▼ Observatories such as this one house huge telescopes. As the Sun sets, the dome slides open and the telescope can be directed at an area of the sky to be studied.

▲ Early peoples did not know why the stars seemed to move, but they observed their patterns. They used the stars to tell the direction when exploring new lands.

WHY ARE HILLS GOOD FOR STARS?
Observatories are often built on hills, because this gives astronomers the best chance for a clear view of the sky and stars.

Early astronomers

In the A.D. 800s, a new school of astronomy was founded in Arabia, and study continued there until the middle of the 1400s. Arab astronomers often drew constellations in human form—such as this one, called Cepheus.

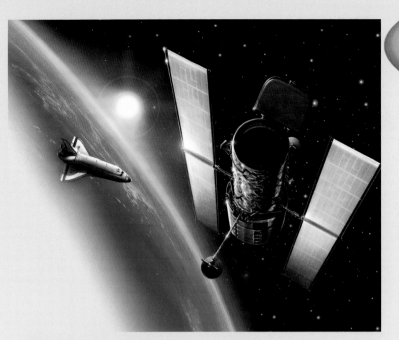

▲ The Hubble space telescope has been orbiting Earth since 1990. Because it is outside our atmosphere, it sends back clearer pictures than we get from any telescope on Earth.

▼ If you want to see more in space, a simple telescope is useful. On a clear night, you will see a lot of stars and constellations.

CREATIVE CORNER

Making your own constellation

Most constellations are made of bright stars that you can see with the naked eye. This one, in the Northern Hemisphere, is called the Big Dipper. Spot a simple shape in the night sky for yourself, draw it on a piece of paper, and give it a name. Now you have your own constellation!

INTERNET LINKS: www.kidsastronomy.com/astroskymap/index.htm • http://www.space.kids.us/hubbletelescope.html

Constellations

There are so many stars in the sky on a clear night that it can be difficult to imagine how people remember them. If you look closely, you will see patterns in the brighter stars. People drew shapes around the patterns and gave them names—these are constellations.

HOW MANY HAVE WE FOUND?

There are 88 official constellations. Newly discovered stars are linked to the constellation that is the closest to them.

▶ Which stars you see depends on where you are in the world and the time of year. In the Northern Hemisphere each season, different constellations can be seen from those seen in the Southern Hemisphere.

Northern Hemisphere

Perseus the hero

The constellation of Perseus was named after a man who found out that his mother was being treated badly by the king. Perseus held up the head of the snake-haired monster Medusa, and the king turned to stone.

▶ The Lynx constellation is named this because you need the eyes of a lynx (a cat) to see its faint shape.

Pegasus

Scorpio

Great Bear

▲ Most constellations are named after figures from myths and legends, including those above. But many recently named constellations, such as the Lynx, are not.

Southern Hemisphere

Ptolemy and the stars
In the A.D. 100s, Roman astronomer Ptolemy grouped more than 1,000 stars into 48 constellations. Although he did not include the stars of the Southern Hemisphere, his star patterns still form the basis for constellations today.

CREATIVE CORNER

The Great Bear game
Copy the stars and lines shown here onto paper. With a counter each and a die, race a friend from the bear's nose to its tail, landing on each star at least once. Visit all four feet first. To win, roll the exact number needed to land on the tip of the tail.

◄ The Southern Cross is a group of four large stars that are easy to recognize in the night sky.

INTERNET LINKS: www.kidsastronomy.com/astroskymap/constellation_hunt.htm

Space travel

The first human-made object to fly into space was a German rocket in 1942. Since then, people have sent many craft, both manned (with a human crew) and unmanned, into space on various missions. These missions have taught us a lot about space and an enormous amount about our Earth and the Moon.

Luna space probes
In 1959, Russia sent three probes to investigate Earth's Moon. *Luna 1* discovered solar wind, *Luna 2* was the first craft to land on the Moon, and *Luna 3* brought back the first images of the far side of the Moon.

◀ For every mission into space, there is a large and experienced ground crew. They monitor equipment and communicate with the computers and people onboard.

▶ Space shuttles such as this one, called *Discovery*, are reusable. They carry equipment and astronauts or cosmonauts to and from space stations and other craft in space.

◀ The *Saturn V* rocket is made up of three parts called stages. When all of their fuel is used, the first and second stages drop away. The third stage continues into space.

CAN YOU FIND?
1. Earth
2. the first stage falling
3. burning fuel from the second stage
4. the third stage
5. a nose cone

VOCABULARY
astronaut
A person trained to travel in a spacecraft.
cosmonaut
A Russian astronaut.
solar wind
A stream of charged particles from the Sun.

▼ It is usual for craft returning to Earth to splash down into an ocean. Parachutes slow them down, and the water cushions their landings much better than land.

Astronauts

It was not until the 1960s that the technology became available to allow people to travel into space. At that time, nobody knew what space travel would do to a human body. Today astronauts know what training they need to survive in space.

Repairing the craft
Astronauts sometimes need to go outside a spacecraft to repair part of it. To do this safely, they wear special suits and breathing equipment and remain securely attached to the craft at all times.

Payload bay

Manipulator arm

Nose cone

Yuri Gagarin
The first person to go into orbit around Earth was Russian astronaut Yuri Gagarin on April 12, 1961. He made one orbit of Earth in a spacecraft called *Vostok 1* before returning to land. The flight lasted for one hour and 48 minutes.

▲ The flight deck and the crew's living space are in the nose cone of a space shuttle. The equipment and other cargo is carried in the payload bay. A manipulator arm loads and unloads the cargo.

◀ Astronauts wear suits called extravehicular mobility units (EMUs) when they need to go outside the spacecraft while they are in orbit. The suits keep them cool as well as provide oxygen and water to drink. They also allow the astronauts to talk with the crew onboard.

HOW DO ASTRONAUTS MOVE IN SPACE?

Astronauts use jet-propelled backpacks called manned maneuvering units (MMUs) to move in space.

▶ All six manned Moon landings collected rock and soil samples. The sixth mission, *Apollo 17*, included a geologist (a scientist who specializes in rocks). He explored the Moon using a lunar roving vehicle.

INTERNET LINKS: www.nasa.gov/audience/forkids/home/F_Best_Dressed_Astronaut.html

Space stations

Space stations are places where people can live and work in space. They are artificial satellites that orbit Earth. Space-station crews may live on a station for weeks or months at a time. Their work includes carrying out scientific experiments and studying the universe from space.

▼ Several countries are working together to build the International Space Station. Crews arrive on a space shuttle with supplies to build the space station.

VOCABULARY
dock
A platform at which a vehicle can unload.
satellite
An object that orbits a planet or star.
solar panels
Panels that take in energy from the Sun.

CAN YOU FIND?
1. solar panels
2. a space shuttle
3. Earth
4. a dock
4. Earth's atmosphere

Salyut, 1971

Skylab, 1973

Mir, 1986

▲ The U.S.S.R. launched the first space station, *Salyut 1*, in 1971. Since then, space stations have grown in size and improved in technology. The International Space Station will be almost one mile wide when it is built.

▲ Some people thought that space stations could be built to look round like a planet. They would then spin and have their own gravity.

▲ Scientists are hoping to build a base on the Moon. From there, they could launch manned craft farther into space— to Mars and possibly more distant planets.

CREATIVE CORNER

Making a model space station

Why not design your own station, using boxes, cardboard tubes, and other empty or unwanted household objects? Remember to include living quarters, docking ports, and solar panels!

Satellites and probes

The first artificial satellite to be launched was *Sputnik 1* in 1957. It was small and sent a signal back to Earth for only three weeks. Today thousands of satellites orbit Earth, including those that we use for television and telephone signals. Each has a different orbit so that they do not crash into one another.

Visiting Venus
In 1962, Venus was the first planet to be reached by a space probe. In 1982, the *Venera 13* probe sent the first color images from the planet. The *Magellan* probe mapped Venus from 1990 to 1994.

Venera 13

▲ Robotic rovers are exploring Mars. They carry equipment, such as cameras and magnets, to collect magnetic dust particles. Their goal is to find evidence of water and a possibility of life on Mars.

▶ In addition to sending pictures and information about other planets, satellites can give us information about Earth as it is seen from space.

▲ In 1997, the *Cassini-Huygens* satellite was launched to study Saturn and its moons and rings. It started orbiting Saturn in 2004 and is still transmitting data.

? WHY DO WE USE PROBES?

Space probes have special instruments that can detect and store information. They can be landed on places where people cannot go.

CREATIVE CORNER

Planning a probe mission

Imagine that you are given the chance to send a probe into space. Where would you send it and what would it look for? Would it bring back samples to Earth? Write a plan outlining your mission, including how long it would take, the type of equipment it would need, and what you would want it to do.

INTERNET LINKS: http://spaceplace.nasa.gov/en/kids/goes/goes_poes_orbits.shtml

Now you know!

▲ The big bang, which most scientists believe formed our universe, happened around 14 billion years ago.

▲ Everything that orbits the Sun is part of our solar system. There may be many other solar systems in the universe.

▲ Earth is the third planet from the Sun. It is farther from it than Mercury and Venus, but closer than Mars.

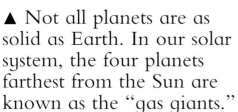

▲ Not all planets are as solid as Earth. In our solar system, the four planets farthest from the Sun are known as the "gas giants."

▲ Comets are small chunks of rocks that orbit the Sun.

▲ To people on Earth, the Moon seems to give off its own light. But it actually only reflects the light of the Sun.

▼ Only a few people have gone into space or set foot on the Moon. Scientists now prefer to use machines or robots to gather information.

▲ Today there are many artificial satellites in space. They send back information to Earth about the planets and stars around us.

Machines

Hundreds of years ago, people were using simple machines on which many of our modern machines are based. Today machines help us in all kinds of ways, and some of the jobs that they do would be impossible for people to do on their own.

What is a machine?

A machine is something that can help us do a job. There are simple machines such as levers, pulleys, gears, and screws. They help us lift heavy weights, alter the direction of a force, or change the force and speed of an object to make it more efficient.

Bar-code reading

Bar codes are found on most things that we buy today. They contain information such as prices. The machine that reads them, a reader, decodes the information.

► Most people who have a bank account get money out of an ATM (automated teller machine). These are usually set in the wall of a building.

Mechanical robots

Robots are machines created to do the type of work that people either cannot or do not want to do. They are often designed to look like humans, although in most cases this is not necessary for the work that they do.

► We use all types of machines to move from one place to another. In general, over land, sea, and air, our means of transportation are getting faster.

Jet Ski

Submersible

▲ Today we can travel fast on an ocean's surface on machines such as a Jet Ski. We are also able to speed through the depths of an ocean in submersibles.

▲ Spacecraft are highly complicated machines that have carried people, animals, and other machines into space. This space shuttle is using a robotic arm to launch a satellite into orbit around the Sun.

▼ The *Sojourner* rover is a special robot built to collect and send back information to Earth from the surface of Mars, where it landed in 1997.

Simple machines

The wheel may be a simple machine, but it is extremely useful to people. Its most obvious use is for transporting people and objects around on land, and we use wheels all the time for this. But we also use wheels as part of other machines such as pulleys and gears. Without wheels, life would be very different!

Wheels through time
The earliest wheels were made of solid wood and were very heavy. Wheels with spokes, such as modern bicycle wheels, were being used around 1500 B.C., and they did not change much from then until air-filled tires were invented in the early 1800s.

► This hammer works as a lever. We push on the handle, and the curve of the hammer changes the direction of the force so that it pulls out the nail.

▼ Tower Bridge in London, England, opens up to let tall ships pass through. In this lever system, the two sections of the bridge that open are counterbalanced by heavy weights. This makes them easier to move.

▲ A baseball bat extends the length of our swing, so we can hit the ball farther. This is also a type of lever.

▶ Cranes are giant levers that can lift heavy weights. We use them to erect tall buildings. You will see cranes at work on construction sites like this one, lifting heavy steel frames into position.

▲ For hundreds of years, people have used animals, such as horses, to pull carriages and carts along on wheels.

◀ Water wheels are powered by the flow of the water in a river. Windmills work in the same way but get their energy from the wind.

VOCABULARY

gear
A disk or wheel that is cut with regular tooth shapes. These engage with teeth in another piece of machinery to make something work.

crane
A machine for lifting and moving heavy weights through the air.

▶ The simplest type of pulley is a single wheel with a groove in its rim. A rope can be pulled down in order to lift something up at the other end.

Pulley

Weight

INTERNET LINKS: www.brainpop.com/technology/simplemachines/pulley/

Bikes and motorcycles

Bicycles were invented just over 200 years ago. They are a cheap and convenient way of getting around faster than people can walk, and they cause very little harm to the environment. Motorcycles are faster than bicycles, but because they use a motor, they are not as kind to the environment.

On one wheel

Unicycles are like bicycles, but with one wheel instead of two. They are more difficult to ride and are popular in circuses. Clowns often teeter around the ring on them to make people laugh.

▼ When motorcyclists take a corner, they need to lean into the bend—or the bike would slip out from underneath them! These racers have protective pads for their elbows and knees.

Tour de France

This is the world's most famous bicycle race. It covers a route around France and sometimes neighboring countries over different terrains. Each year it alternates between a clockwise and a counterclockwise route.

► Speed cycling is an Olympic sport. The riders compete in a stadium shaped like a bowl, with steep sides that help them go faster.

▲ Mountain bikes have many gears to help climb hills and tires that grip well. But if the going gets tough, sometimes walking is the only way to move forward!

HOW FAST CAN THEY GO?
The fastest motorcycles can reach speeds of more than 347 mph (560km/h)—and designers keep making them faster!

► There are stunt motorcyclists who can perform amazing tricks. They often jump over rows of buses or trucks.

► Designs where the rider lies back in his or her seat (like this tricycle) can go faster than many upright bicycles or tricycles. Their streamlined shape helps them travel more easily.

INTERNET LINKS: www.pedalinghistory.com/PHhistory.html • www.factmonster.com/ipka/A0933211.html

Cars, buses, and trucks

Most cars are designed to carry a small number of people on trips to school or work, on vacation, and for shopping. Buses carry many more people. They are more economical than cars, and most are better for the environment. Trucks are mostly used to carry heavy materials rather than people.

Taller than a man
Some of the biggest tires in the world are made for dump trucks. They carry heavy loads around construction sites, and the tires help cushion the weight.

▶ Our towns and cities are packed with cars and other vehicles. Many countries have had to build more and wider roads to prevent traffic from building up.

▲ Cars travel from factories where they are made to showrooms to be sold. They are carried on car transporters.

Beetle story
The Volkswagen Beetle is probably the most easily recognized car in the world. It was designed and built in the 1900s as a car for ordinary people. Its name comes from people thinking that it looked like a beetle.

▲ Trucks of all types move products long distances. Some, like this one, can tip up their containers to deliver goods.

Bus

Bus

▲ Trams, like buses, are a type of public transportation. They run on rails on the ground, but they get electric power from cables above them.

▲ People travel on all types of vehicles. The bus on top is from Ecuador. The U.S. bus above is more comfortable.

CAN YOU FIND?
1. an ambulance
2. firefighters
3. a stretcher
4. a lifting platform
5. a hose pipe

▼ Fire engines are equipped with all types of emergency equipment. The long, cranelike arm can move the firefighters close to the center of a fire to put it out quickly.

124

Building machines

All types of machines are used on construction sites, including diggers, dump trucks, bulldozers, rollers, and pavers. Each of them has a special job to do. All of these machines are designed to work hard and keep the people who operate them safe.

▼ Today we dig, or bore, tunnels with huge digging machines. A large, round cutting head at the front cuts into the rock or soil, and behind it the tunnel is lined with material such as concrete.

Preparing a site
Bulldozers clear the ground so that it is flat enough to build on. A sharp blade at the front of the bucket cuts through whatever is in the way. A bulldozer is a lot like a giant lawn mower!

▲ On a busy construction site, there are many different jobs. Surveyors measure the site and engineers check that it is safe. Demolition cranes knock down old buildings.

◄ Hammer drills like this break up the ground quickly, but they are very noisy. Workers on the site need to wear ear protectors to safeguard their hearing.

◄ Bridges help us cross obstacles such as rivers. They are usually built of heavy materials, such as concrete and steel, and are lifted into place by cranes and other machines.

► In road building, dump trucks move materials from one place to another. Graders make the ground smooth.

Dump truck

Grader

Roller

Paver

◄ Paver machines lay the surface of the road, while heavy rollers follow behind them, flattening and leveling the surface.

▲ Giant bulldozers can cut through and clear large amounts of rubble and waste very quickly.

CREATIVE CORNER

Building-words game

Think of a word or phrase about building vehicles such as "bulldozer." Write down any other words that you can make out of the letters in five minutes. Play against a friend. Score one point for each correctly spelled word.

Trains

Trains run on rails, carrying people and goods on short or long overland journeys. They are a cheaper form of transportation than cars and are kinder to the environment. Many people use trains to commute, or travel, to work in cities and towns, and most large cities have at least one major railroad station.

▲ Most trains run on tracks with two rails for stability. But monorails (above) have only one rail.

◄ Australia's Katoomba Scenic Railway was built in the 1800s for use in mining. Since the 1930s, it has been used for tourists.

► Trains, like cars, need signals so that the driver knows when it is safe to move on. A red light means "stop," and a green light means "go."

The golden spike
In the 1800s, two railroads were joined to create the first railroad that crossed the U.S. from one coast to another. The last spike to be driven in was a golden one to mark the ceremony.

► Goods trains often use the same tracks as passenger trains, but may travel at night, when the tracks would otherwise be quiet or even empty. These trains are an efficient way of transporting goods.

▼ In a large, modern city, railroad stations often link overground and underground (subway) railroad lines. They also connect to airport terminals and give access to public and private road transportation. They may be built on several different levels, connected by stairs, escalators, and elevators.

CAN YOU FIND?
1. a subway train
2. an escalator
3. a tram
4. a monorail
5. an overground train
6. a ticket office

▲ Some steam engines, such as this one in the Rocky Mountains, are still used today and are popular with tourists.

Ships and boats

Our ancestors would have used small boats for fishing and sailing on rivers and streams. As they found ways of making bigger and better boats, they used them for traveling farther and finding new places to live. Today's ships are packed with technology and safety devices.

Paddleboats
These types of boats were one of the earliest mechanically powered boats, and they are still popular today. A steam engine drives the large wheel, or paddle, on the stern. This pushes the boat forward.

◀ Inflatable boats, like this rubber raft, are light and easy to transport. They are often used on rivers and lakes.

▶ Ocean liners are popular for traveling long distances, and the cruise industry is growing. These large ships carry thousands of passengers and crew. There is onboard entertainment for the passengers.

The sinking of the *Titanic*
The *Titanic* was a huge passenger and mail ship. It was said to be unsinkable. But on its maiden (first) voyage from Southampton, England, to New York City in 1912, it hit an iceberg and split in half.

▲ Hovercraft travel on a cushion of air, which is produced by a large fan. This makes a hovercraft float above both land and water.

VOCABULARY

hull
The hollow, main body of a boat or ship. It floats partly underwater.

stern
The rear section of a ship or boat.

▲ Motorboats are small, fast boats with powerful engines. People use them for racing or just for the thrill of traveling fast over the water.

▼ No matter how safe boats become, the sea is always unpredictable and therefore dangerous. Lifeboats are ready at all times to rescue people who are in trouble.

► Catamarans are boats that have two hulls. They can be powered either by sails or engines. Catamarans are generally faster and more stable than single-hulled boats.

Aircraft

Airplanes travel faster than ships, cars, and trains. This is partly because they can fly over obstacles rather than having to go around them. Also, air slows down objects less than water and land do. Nevertheless, to get off the ground at all, aircraft need powerful engines and specially designed wings to provide lift.

▼ Modern airports have planes taking off and landing all the time. Some large airports have more than 1,000 planes landing every day! Buses, trains, and trucks carry people, luggage, and other goods around the site.

First flight
The first time an airplane flew with a pilot onboard was in 1903. Orville Wright flew the "Flyer," an airplane that he and his brother, Wilbur, had designed. It flew for 121 ft. (37m) and was in the air for only 12 seconds before it landed again.

▲ Stealth bombers like this one are so named because they absorb and reflect radar. This makes them difficult to detect.

WHO INVENTED FLYING?
No one really knows. However, there are many ancient stories about people using kites or wings.

▲ Airships contain a gas, such as helium, that is lighter than air. But they also have engines to power them.

▲ Jump jets are designed to be able to take off and land on very short runways. They are even able to take off from the deck of a ship.

▲ Gliders don't have engines. The pilots have to find pockets of warm, rising air called thermals to stay up in the air.

▲ Helicopters take off vertically. They are used where other aircraft cannot land or take off.

▲ Small planes are often used when a few people need to travel quickly over long distances. They are often used to reach remote places.

CREATIVE CORNER

Making a glider
1. Take a piece of 8 ½ x 11-in. paper. Fold one end back so that it is roughly square. **2.** Now fold in the corners as shown. **3.** Crease along the center line and then fold the wings out again. **4.** Now you are ready to launch your glider!

1.

2.

3.

4.

Machines at work

Machines are useful in all types of work situations, from factories and farms to offices and construction sites. We use machines for almost every task that we do, as they can do both light and heavy work. We are inventing new machines to help us do our jobs all the time.

▲ Using a milking machine to milk cows is quick and easy. It saves time compared to doing it by hand, as people used to do.

Robot paint sprayer
In car factories, the body of a car is spray-painted by machines. Today the machines are often robots that work automatically. The machines are carefully controlled to spray an even layer of paint on each part of the car.

▲ Snowblowers remove snow from roads and other places where it is not wanted. These road machines are powered by electricity or an engine. They blow the snow out of the way or into a truck that carries it away.

▶ Most offices use computers, photocopiers, telephones, and printers. Computers help us communicate, calculate numbers, plan our work, and design all types of things, from the pages of a book to a towering office building.

◀ Paper is made on huge pieces of machinery. Many are the length of two soccer fields. They can produce giant rolls of paper, like those shown here, at up to 6,600 ft. (2,000m) per minute.

▲ TV studios use many types of machinery. They have cameras, microphones, lighting, and sometimes teleprompters, from which the host or actor reads the script.

CREATIVE CORNER

Making a spool motor

Thread a rubber band through a spool of thread. Loop one end around an eraser and the other end around a pencil. Wind up the rubber band by turning the pencil. Add a blob of modeling clay or tape a coin to the pencil, place the spool onto the floor, and watch it go!

Machines in the home

Even in our homes, we use many machines to help us with all types of tasks. A modern home often includes machines that cook, wash, and clean for us. Other machines heat or cool the air so that we are comfortable. Even more keep us entertained.

Robot helpers

Designers are working hard to produce small, efficient robots that can perform tasks around the house. They could even clean and operate the other machines.

CAN YOU FIND?

1. a washing machine
2. a toaster
3. a food processor
4. a microwave oven
5. a refrigerator

▼ Today's kitchens are full of machinery. Most of them run on electricity or gas. Microwave ovens are a good, energy-saving alternative for cooking.

▼ A modern bedroom uses a lot of electricity. Televisions, computers, lighting, radios, and CD players all run on it. They either are plugged into wall outlets or use batteries.

▲ Sewing machines allow us to make and alter clothes much more quickly than we can by hand.

▶ Vacuum cleaners make it much easier to keep our floors clean.

▲ Many of us own special machines that are designed for personal use. These include music players, cameras, and video-game consoles.

CREATIVE CORNER

Making a poster
Collect pictures of machines that you find in the home and sort them into groups to put on a poster—for example, some that help you prepare food. Glue them onto a piece of paper and label each group.

Food machines

Hospitals and health

Modern hospitals use a large range of machines. Some help medical staff find out what is wrong with a patient by testing for different diseases and symptoms. Others are used to treat illnesses. The staff have to be trained to use the machines correctly and to understand all of the information that they provide.

▲ Sometimes surgeons need to operate in order to make someone better. This is done in an operating room while the patient is asleep.

WHAT IS BLOOD PRESSURE?

It is the amount of pressure of the blood on the walls of the arteries. Either too much or too little pressure is bad for your health.

▲ Blood pressure can be measured accurately on a machine. It tells us if our blood pressure is too high or too low.

▶ Hospitals often have an area with special fitness machines, which patients can use to get in shape after an illness. Different machines are designed to allow people to exercise different parts of their bodies.

▲ People who have an injury or suddenly become sick may be taken to an emergency room in a hospital. They may travel in an ambulance that is full of special machinery to keep them as stable as possible until they arrive.

▲ Special scanners use x-rays to look at what is going on inside a patient's body. Doctors use the resulting scans to decide on the best treatment.

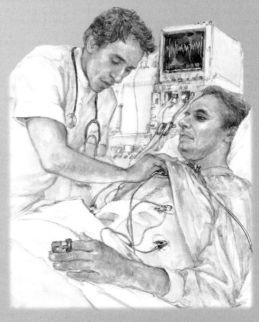

▲ This patient's heart is being monitored. The steady heartbeats are displayed on the monitor next to his bed.

INTERNET LINKS: www.knowitall.org/kidswork/hospital/history/modern/index.html

Now you know!

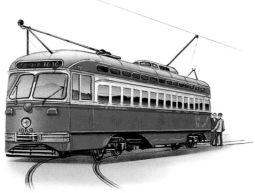

▶ Catamarans are boats with two hulls.

▲ Robots are often designed to look like humans, although in most cases this is not necessary for the work that they do.

▲ Trams run on rails on the ground, but they get their electric power from cables above them.

▶ Stunt motorcyclists perform amazing tricks such as jumping over buses and trucks.

▲ Paper-making machines produce giant rolls of paper at up to 6,600 ft. (2,000m) per minute.

▲ Australia's Katoomba Scenic Railway was originally built in the 1800s for use in mining.

▲ Trains that run on one rail are called monorails.

▲ Hospitals often have a fitness area for patients to use to get back in shape after an illness.

Index

Acknowledgments

The publisher would like to thank the following illustrators:
Jonathan Adams, Julian Baum, Mark Bergin, Robin Boutell, Peter Bull, Robin Carter, Kuo Kang Chen, Peter Dennis (Linda Rogers), Richard Draper, Angelina Elsebach, Dianne Fawcett, James Field (Simon Girling & Associates), Chris Forsey, Terry Gabbey (AFA Ltd.), Ruby Green, Terry Hadler, Tim Hayward (Bernard Thornton Artists), Christian Hook, Richard Hook, Biz Hull, Ian Jackson (Wildlife Art), Michael Johnson, Deborah Kindred (Simon Girling), Stuart Lafford, Terence Lambert, Stephen Lings, Patricia Ludlow, Chris Lyon, Kevin Maddison, Maltings Partners, David McAllister, Steve Noon (Garden Studio), Nicki Palin, Sebastien Quigley (Linden Artists), Bernard Robinson, Eric Roe, Mike Rowe, Elizabeth Sawyer (SGA), Rob Shone, Guy Smith (Mainline Design), Roger Stewart, Gareth Williams, David Wright (Kathy Jakeman)

Creative Corner illustrations throughout: Jo Moore